# Experiencing

INTERMEDIATE

# Choral Music

## SIGHT-SINGING

Developed by

HAL•LEONARD® CORPORATION

 Glencoe

New York, New York    Columbus, Ohio    Chicago, Illinois    Peoria, Illinois    Woodland Hills, California

 **Glencoe**

The **McGraw·Hill** Companies

Printed in the United States of America.

Send all inquiries to:
Glencoe/McGraw-Hill
21600 Oxnard Street, Suite 500
Woodland Hills, CA  91367

ISBN 0-07-861117-2

2 3 4 5 6 7 8 9   045   09 08 07 06 05 04

# Credits

## AUTHORS

**Emily Crocker**
Vice President of Choral Publications
Hal Leonard Corporation, Milwaukee, Wisconsin
Founder and Artistic Director, Milwaukee Children's Choir

**Audrey Snyder**
Composer
Eugene, Oregon

## EDITORIAL

**Linda Rann**
Senior Editor
Hal Leonard Corporation, Milwaukee, Wisconsin

**Stacey Nordmeyer**
Choral Editor
Hal Leonard Corporation, Milwaukee, Wisconsin

# Table of Contents

# TO THE STUDENT

**Welcome to choir!**

By singing in the choir, you have chosen to be a part of an exciting and rewarding adventure. The benefits of being in choir are many. Basically, singing is fun. It provides an expressive way of sharing your feelings and emotions. Through choir, you will have friends that share a common interest with you. You will experience the joy of making beautiful music together. Choir provides an opportunity to develop interpersonal skills. It takes teamwork and cooperation to sing together, and you must learn how to work with others. As you critique your individual and group performances, you can improve your ability to analyze and communicate your thoughts clearly.

Even if you do not pursue a music career, music can be an important part of your life. There are many avocational opportunities in music. **Avocational** means *not related to a job or career.* Singing as a hobby can provide you with personal enjoyment, enrich your life, and teach you life skills. Singing is something you can do for the rest of your life.

In this course, you will be presented with the basic skills of music notation and sight-singing. You will learn new concepts through exercises, combinable lines, speech choruses and original sight-singing practice songs. Guidelines for becoming a successful choir member include:

- Come to class prepared to learn.
- Respect the efforts of others.
- Work daily to improve your sight-singing skills.
- Sing expressively at all times.
- Have fun singing.

This book was written to provide you with a meaningful choral experience. Take advantage of the knowledge and opportunities offered here. Your exciting adventure of experiencing choral music is about to begin!

# CHAPTER 1

# Rhythm

## ◆ The Beat

Just as the heart beats with an even pulse, the **beat** is *the steady pulse of all music.*

## ◆ Quarter Note and Quarter Rest

Composers assign music notes and rests to represent the beat. In this case, a **quarter note** is *a note that represents one beat of sound* and a **quarter rest** is *a rest that represents one beat of silence.*

Quarter Note                    Quarter Rest

## ◆ Practice

Clap, tap or chant the following exercises to practice reading quarter notes and quarter rests. Keep the beat steady.

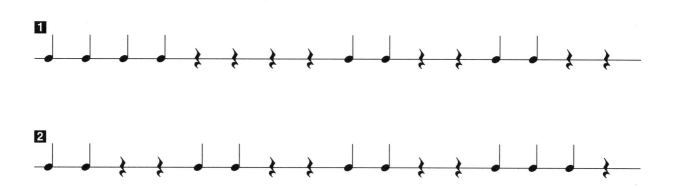

# Terms and Symbols

### ◆ Barline and Measure

In music, a **barline** is *a vertical line that groups notes and rests together.* A **measure** is *the space between two barlines.*

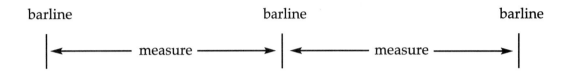

Any number of beats can be grouped in a measure. In the exercise below, there are four beats per measure. Clap, tap or chant the rhythm, keeping the beat steady.

# Rhythm

### ◆ Time Signature • $\frac{4}{4}$ Meter

**Meter** is *a way of organizing rhythm.* A **time signature** (sometimes called a meter signature) is *the set of numbers at the beginning of a piece of music.*

$\frac{4}{4}$ **meter** is *a time signature in which there are four beats per measure and the quarter note receives the beat.*

**4** The top number indicates the number of beats per measure.
**4** The bottom number indicates the kind of note that receives the beat.

Clap, tap or chant the following exercise to practice reading rhythmic patterns in four.

# Pitch

## ◆ The Staff

A **staff** is *a series of five horizontal lines and four spaces on which notes are written.* Notes are placed on a staff to indicate **pitch**, or *how high or low each note sounds.* A staff is like a ladder. Notes placed higher on the staff sound higher than notes placed lower on the staff.

higher pitch                              lower pitch

Staff

## ◆ Treble Clef and Bass Clef

A **clef** is *the symbol at the beginning of a staff that indicates which lines and spaces represent which notes.* A **treble clef** is *a clef that generally indicates notes that sound higher than middle C.* A **bass clef** is *a clef that generally indicates notes that sound lower than middle C.*

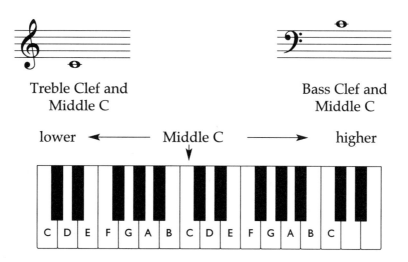

Treble Clef and          Bass Clef and
Middle C                 Middle C

## ◆ The Grand Staff

A **grand staff** is *a staff that is created when two staves are joined together.* Again, the higher a note is placed on the staff, the higher its pitch. The lower a note is placed on the staff, the lower its pitch.

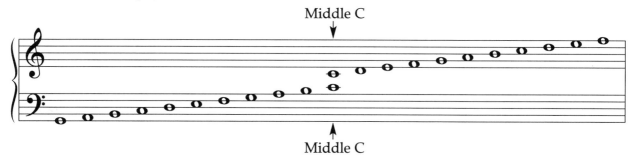

# Pitch

## ◆ The Scale

A **scale** is *a group of notes that are sung or played in succession and are based on a particular home tone, or keynote.* Here are two ways to visualize a scale.

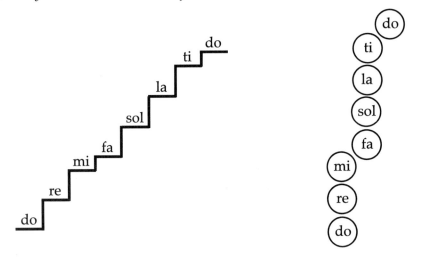

## ◆ Key

In a scale, the **key** is *determined by its home tone, or keynote.* For example, in the key of C major, C is the home tone. Sing the scale below.

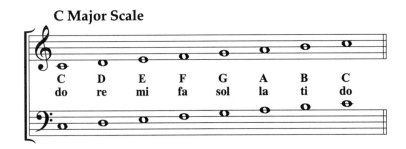

## ◆ Practice

Adjusting to fit your vocal range, read and echo the following exercises to practice singing notes from the C major scale.

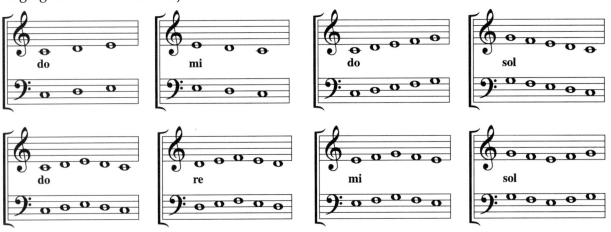

# Rhythm

The **beat** is *the steady pulse of all music*. **Rhythm** is *the combination of long and short notes and rests*. These may move with the beat, faster than the beat or slower than the beat.

## ◆ Half Note and Half Rest

A **half note** is *a note that represents two beats of sound when the quarter note receives the beat.* A **half rest** is *a rest that represents two beats of silence when the quarter note receives the beat.*

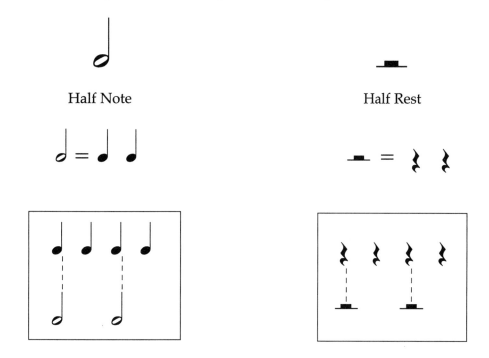

Half Note                                        Half Rest

## ◆ Practice

Clap, tap or chant the following exercises to practice reading half notes and half rests.

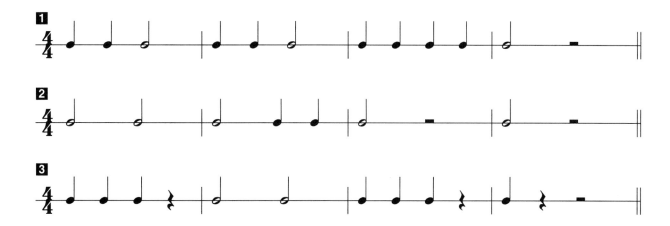

# Rhythm

## ◆ Time Signature • $\frac{4}{4}$ Meter

$\frac{4}{4}$ **meter** is *a time signature in which there are four beats per measure and the quarter note receives the beat.*

**4** = four beats per measure

**4** = the quarter note receives the beat

Study and practice the conducting pattern to the right.

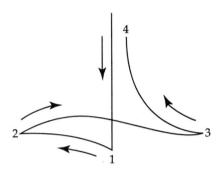

## ◆ Practice

Chant the rhythms in the following exercises as you conduct.

**1**

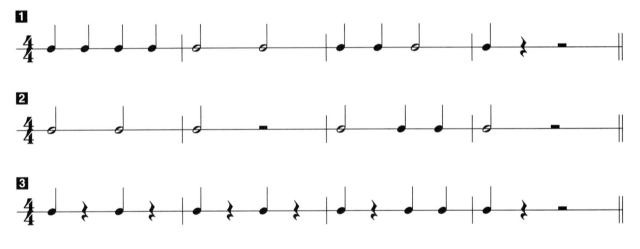

**2**

**3**

**4**

**5**

## ◆ Common Time • ₵

**Common time**, or common meter, is *another name for* $\frac{4}{4}$ *meter.* Clap, tap or chant the following exercise to practice reading rhythmic patterns in common time.

**6**

# Practice

## ◆ Pitch and Rhythm • C Major

Now read pitch and rhythm together. Using notes from the C major scale below as a guide, sight-sing the following exercises by first clapping or chanting the rhythm. Then, speak the pitch names using **solfège syllables** *(do, re, mi)*. Finally, sing each exercise using solfège syllables. After singing each exercise separately, combine them in two, three or more parts.

## ◆ Challenge

Conduct in four while you sing.

# Rhythm

## ◆ Dotted Half Note

A **dotted half note** is *a note that represents three beats of sound when the quarter note receives the beat.* Three beats of rests are represented by ▬ ╏ or ╏ ▬ .

Dotted Half Note                    Three Beats of Rests

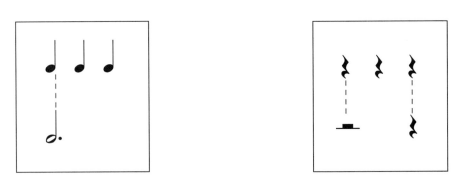

## ◆ Practice

Clap, tap or chant the following exercises to practice reading dotted half notes.

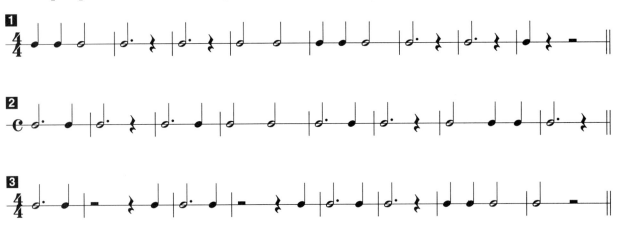

# Rhythm

### ◆ Whole Note and Whole Rest

A **whole note** is *a note that represents four beats of sound when the quarter note receives the beat.* A **whole rest** is *a rest that represents four beats of silence when the quarter note receives the beat.* In $\frac{4}{4}$ meter, a whole note represents one full measure of sound, and a whole rest represents one full measure of silence.

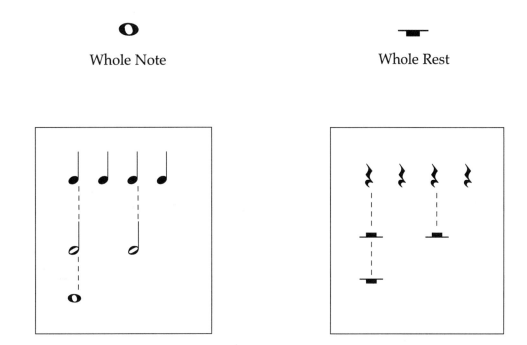

Whole Note                                                    Whole Rest

### ◆ Practice

Clap, tap or chant the following exercises to practice reading whole notes and whole rests.

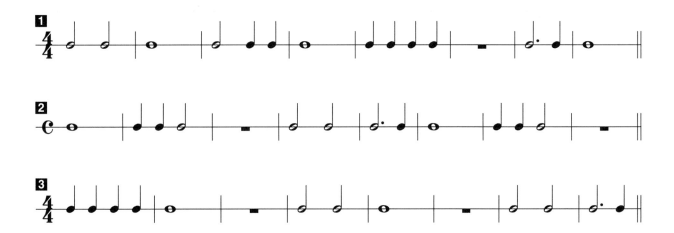

# Practice

◆ Pitch and Rhythm • C Major

Using the notes from the C major scale below as a guide, sight-sing the following exercises separately or in any combination.

◆ Challenge

Conduct in four while you sing.

# Terms and Symbols

## ◆ Double Barline ‖

A **double barline** is *a set of two barlines that indicate the end of a piece or section of music.* The end of a piece of music may also be labeled "fine" (*FEE-nay*).

## ◆ Practice

Adjusting to fit your vocal range, sight-sing the following exercises.

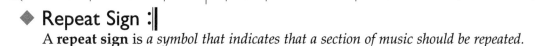

## ◆ Repeat Sign :‖

A **repeat sign** is *a symbol that indicates that a section of music should be repeated.*

## ◆ Practice

Adjusting to fit your vocal range, sight-sing the following exercises, observing the repeat signs.

# A Song For Today

Words and Music by
AUDREY SNYDER

# Evaluation

Demonstrate what you have learned in Chapter One by completing the following:

◆ Name the first five notes of the C major scale.

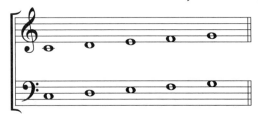

◆ **4** What does the top number mean in this time signature?

   **4** What does the bottom number mean?

◆ Name these kinds of notes and rests:

◆ In $\frac{4}{4}$ meter:
    1. One half note equals the same amount of time as how many quarter notes?
    2. One dotted half note equals the same amount of time as how many quarter notes?
    3. A whole note receives how many beats?

◆ Sight-sing the following exercises.

# CHAPTER 2

# Pitch

## ◆ The C Major Scale

A **scale** is *a group of notes that are sung or played in succession and are based on a particular home tone, or keynote.*

Play a scale on the piano starting on C and ending on C, using only the white notes and without skipping any notes.

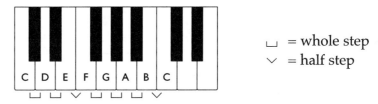

⊔ = whole step
∨ = half step

These notes form a pattern of whole steps and half steps. A **half step** is *the smallest distance between two notes.* A **whole step** is *the combination of two half steps side by side.*

The **major scale** is *a scale that has* do *as its home tone, or keynote.* It is made up of a specific arrangement of whole steps and half steps in the following order:

W + W + H + W + W + W + H

Sing the C major scale using solfège syllables. Where do the whole steps occur? Where do the half steps occur?

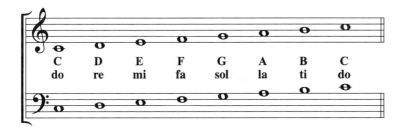

## ◆ Practice

Adjusting to fit your vocal range, read and echo the following exercises to practice singing notes from the C major scale.

# Practice

## ◆ Pitch and Rhythm • C Major in $\frac{4}{4}$ Meter

Using the C major scale below as a guide, sight-sing the following exercises by first clapping or chanting the rhythms. Then, speak the pitch names using solfège syllables. Finally, sing each exercise using solfège syllables. After singing each exercise separately, combine them in two, three or more parts.

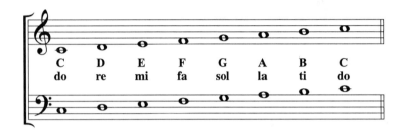

## ◆ Challenge

Conduct in four while you sing.

# Rhythm

### ◆ Time Signature • $\frac{3}{4}$ Meter

$\frac{3}{4}$ **meter** is *a time signature in which there are three beats per measure and the quarter note receives the beat.* A whole rest ▬ in $\frac{3}{4}$ meter represents one measure of silence.

**4** = four beats per measure
**4** = the quarter note receives the beat

**3** = three beats per measure
**4** = the quarter note receives the beat

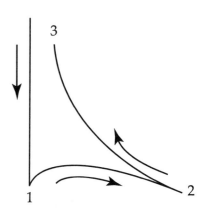

Study and practice the conducting pattern to the right.

### ◆ Practice

Chant the rhythms in the following exercises as you conduct.

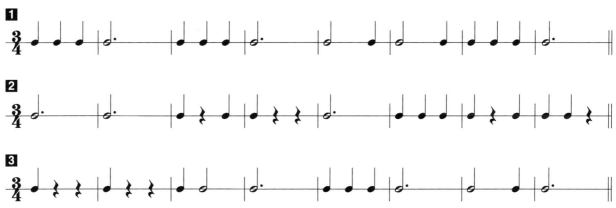

Sight-sing the following exercises separately or in any combination.

# Lazy Afternoon

Words and Music by
EMILY CROCKER

# Pitch

### ◆ The A Minor Scale

The major scale is a specific arrangement of whole steps and half steps:

$$W + W + H + W + W + W + H$$

The C major scale is a major scale that starts and ends on C. The half steps occur between E and F *(mi and fa)* and B and C *(ti and do).*

Play a scale on the piano starting on A and ending on A, using only the white notes and without skipping any notes. Notice how different it sounds from a major scale.

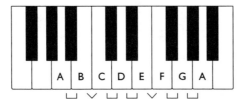

⎵ = whole step

∨ = half step

The **minor scale** is *a scale that has la as its home tone, or keynote.* It is made up of a specific arrangement of whole steps and half steps in the following order:

$$W + H + W + W + H + W + W$$

Sing the A minor scale using solfège syllables. Where do the whole steps occur? Where do the half steps occur?

The A minor scale is called the relative minor of the C major scale since both scales have the same half steps (E and F, *mi and fa*; B and C, *ti and do*).

### ◆ Practice

Adjusting to fit your vocal range, read and echo the following exercises to practice singing notes from the A minor scale.

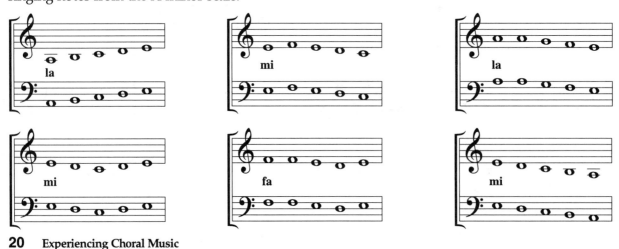

# Practice

◆ Pitch and Rhythm • A Minor in $\frac{3}{4}$ Meter

Using the A minor scale below as a guide, sight-sing the following exercises separately or in any combination.

**A Minor Scale**

**1**

**2**

**3**

**4**

**5**

**6**

◆ Challenge

Conduct in three while you sing.

# Spanish Guitar

Words and Music by
EMILY CROCKER

# Evaluation

Demonstrate what you have learned in Chapter Two by completing the following:

◆ Name the notes in the C major and A minor scales. Sing them using solfège syllables. Where are the half steps in each scale?

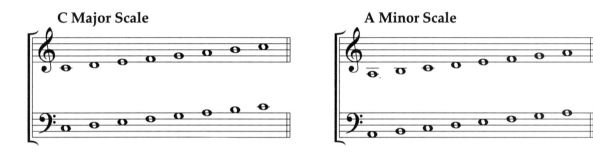

C Major Scale          A Minor Scale

◆ Sight-sing the following melodies.

Three to Get Ready

la

Four to Go

do

## ◆ Be A Composer

Copy the rhythm below on a sheet of paper. Choose pitches from the C major scale for each note, then transfer them to a music staff. (You may want to start and end your melody on *do* or C.) Sing your melody using solfège syllables. Play your melody on a keyboard or create words for your melody.

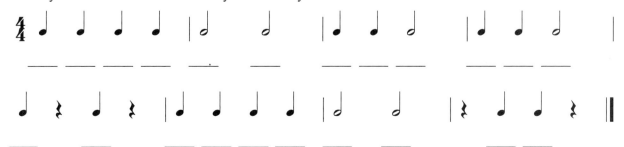

# CHAPTER 3

# Rhythm

## ◆ Eighth Notes

The **beat** is *the steady pulse of all music.* **Rhythm** is *the combination of long and short notes and rests.*

An **eighth note** is *a note that represents half a beat of sound when the quarter note receives the beat.* Two eighth notes equal one beat of sound when the quarter note receives the beat.

Eighth Notes

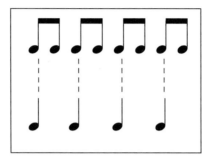

## ◆ Practice

Clap, tap or chant while conducting the following exercises to practice reading eighth notes.

# Rhythm

## ◆ Eighth Rest

An **eighth rest** is *a rest that represents half a beat of silence when the quarter note receives the beat.*

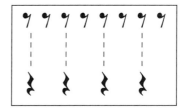

Eighth Rest

## ◆ Practice

Clap, tap or chant the following exercises to practice reading eighth notes and eighth rests.

## ◆ Grouping Eighth Notes

Eighth notes can be beamed together in groups, or they can be separated into single notes.

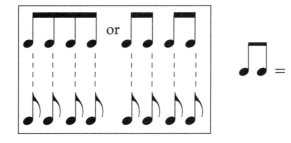

## ◆ Practice

Clap, tap or chant the following exercises to practice reading eighth notes and eighth rests.

# Pitch

## ◆ The C Major Tonic Chord

A **chord** is *the combination of three or more notes played or sung at the same time.* The **tonic chord** is *a chord built on the home tone, or keynote, of a scale.*

In a major scale, the tonic chord uses the notes *do, mi* and *sol.* This chord may be called the **I** ("one") chord, since it is based on the first note of the scale, or *do.*

C Major Tonic Chord

## ◆ Practice

An **interval** is *the distance between two notes.* Adjusting to fit your vocal range, read and echo the following exercises to practice singing intervals found in the C major tonic chord.

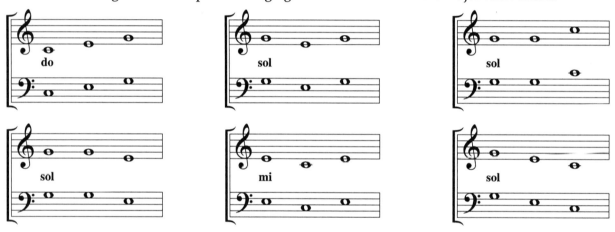

Adjusting to fit your vocal range, sight-sing the following exercises that use pitches found in the C major tonic chord.

# Practice

### ◆ Pitch and Rhythm • C Major in $\frac{4}{4}$ Meter

Using the C major patterns below as a guide, sight-sing the following exercises by first clapping or chanting the rhythms. Then, speak the pitch names using solfège syllables. Finally, sing each example using solfège syllables. After singing each exercise separately, combine them in two, three or more parts.

### ◆ Challenge

Conduct in four while you sing.

# Black Cat

Words and Music by
AUDREY SNYDER

# Rhythm

## ◆ Tied Notes

A **tie** is *a curved line used to connect two or more notes of the same pitch in order to make one longer note.*

## ◆ Practice

Sight-sing the following exercises that use tied notes.

# Pitch

### ◆ The A Minor Tonic Chord

A **chord** is *the combination of three or more notes played or sung at the same time.* The **tonic chord** is *a chord built on the home tone, or keynote, of a scale.*

In a minor scale, the tonic chord uses the notes *la, do* and *mi.* This chord may be called the **i** ("one") chord, since it is based on the first note of the scale, or *la.*

A Minor Tonic Chord

### ◆ Practice

Adjusting to fit your vocal range, read and echo the following exercises to practice singing intervals found in the A minor tonic chord.

Adjusting to fit your vocal range, sight-sing the following exercises that use pitches found in the A minor tonic chord.

# Practice

◆ Pitch and Rhythm • A Minor in $\frac{3}{4}$ and $\frac{4}{4}$ Meter

Using the A minor patterns below as a guide, sight-sing the following sets of exercises separately or in any combination.

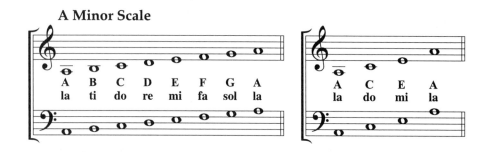

**A Minor Scale**

Exercises in $\frac{3}{4}$ Meter

Exercises in $\frac{4}{4}$ Meter

# Autumn Delight

Words and Music by
AUDREY SNYDER

coax - ing the branch - es to share their au - tumn de - light.

tic - ing the branch - es to share their au - tumn de - light.

**21**

*cresc.*

Let - ting go, _____ red and gold, _____ leaves are joy - ful - ly _____ danc - ing

*cresc.*

Let - ting go, red and gold, joy - ful - ly danc - ing

*cresc.*

**29**

*f*

*mf*

free. _____ High in the trees the wind rus - tles

*f*

free. _____

*f*

*mf*

# Evaluation

Demonstrate what you have learned in Chapter Three by completing the following:

◆ Name the notes in the following chords and sing them using solfège syllables.

**C Major Tonic Chord**

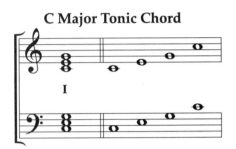

**A Minor Tonic Chord**

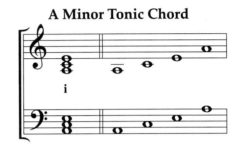

◆ When the quarter note receives the beat, how many beats are there in each of the tied note combinations below?

◆ Sight-sing the following exercises.

# CHAPTER 4

# Pitch

## ◆ The F Major Scale

A **flat** (♭) is *a symbol that lowers the pitch of a given note one half step.*
The note to the right, B♭ (B flat), is written with the flat sign to the left of
the notehead.

The major scale is a specific arrangement of whole steps and half steps: W + W +
H + W + W + W + H

The F major scale is a major scale that starts and ends on F. To build this scale, begin
on F and use the pattern of whole steps and half steps shown above. Notice the need for
a B♭. Play the F major scale on the piano.

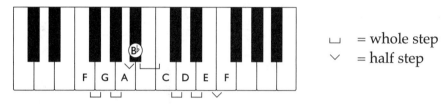

Sing the F major scale using solfège syllables. Where do the whole steps occur?
Where do the half steps occur?

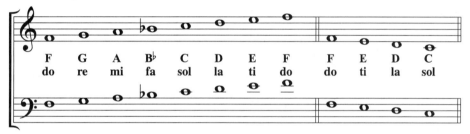

## ◆ Key Signature

The **key signature** is *a symbol or set of symbols that determines the key of a piece of music.*
In the key of F major, there will always be a B♭. Rather than write a flat sign on every B in
a piece of music, a flat is placed on the B line on the staff at the beginning of the piece, to
the right of the clef sign.

The key signature for F major looks like this:

## ◆ Practice

Read and echo the following examples to practice singing notes from the F major scale.

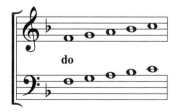

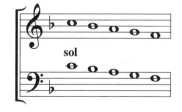

# Practice

## ◆ Pitch and Rhythm • F Major in $\frac{4}{4}$ Meter

Using the F major patterns below as a guide, sight-sing the following exercises separately or in any combination.

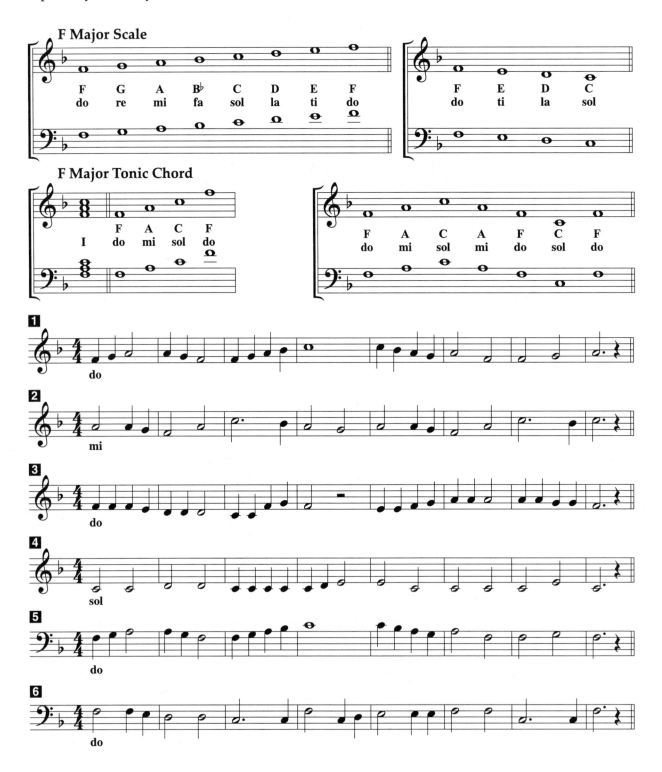

# Sing All Together

Words and Music by
EMILY CROCKER

# Rhythm

◆ **Reviewing Tied Notes**

A **tie** is *a curved line used to connect two or more notes of the same pitch in order to make one longer note.* For example, two quarter notes tied together equal one half note.

◆ **Practice**

Clap, tap, or chant while conducting the following exercises that use tied notes.

**1**

**2**

**3**

**4**

Sight-sing the following exercises that use tied notes.

**5**

do

**6**

do

# Rhythm

## ◆ Dotted Half and Dotted Quarter Notes

A **dot** is *a symbol that increases the length of a given note by half its value.* It is placed to the right of the note.

When the quarter note receives the beat:

A dotted half note receives three beats (the same as a half note tied to a quarter note).

A dotted quarter note receives one and a half beats (the same as a quarter note tied to an eighth note).

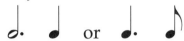

Dotted rhythms are often combinations of unequal note values. For example, a longer dotted note is sometimes followed by a shorter note.

## ◆ Practice

Clap, tap or chant while conducting the following exercises that use dotted half and dotted quarter notes.

Sight-sing the following exercises that use dotted half and dotted quarter notes.

# Terms and Symbols

## ◆ Dynamics

Sight-sing and practice this two-part speech chorus. Make your performance more interesting by using **dynamics,** or *symbols in music used to indicate how loud or soft to sing.* See the box on the right for a quick guide to dynamics.

| | |
|---|---|
| *p* | = piano (soft) |
| *mp* | = mezzo piano (medium soft) |
| *mf* | = mezzo forte (medium loud) |
| *f* | = forte (loud) |
| *ff* | = fortissimo (very loud) |
| < | = crescendo (get louder) |
| > | = decrescendo (get softer) |

**SIGHT-SING**

# Hitch It, Ditch It

Words and Music by
EMILY CROCKER

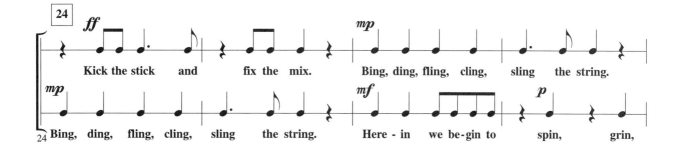

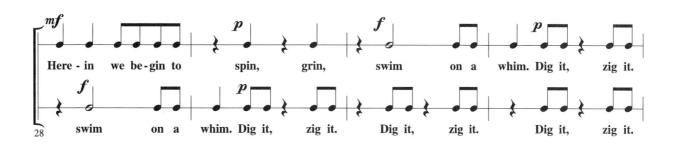

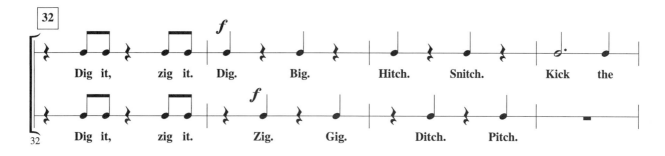

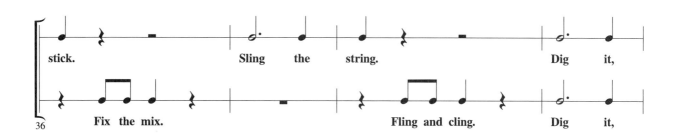

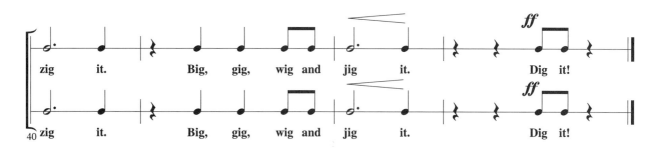

# Practice

◆ Pitch and Rhythm • Dotted Notes in $\frac{4}{4}$ Meter

Using the F major patterns below as a guide, sight-sing the following exercises separately or in any combination.

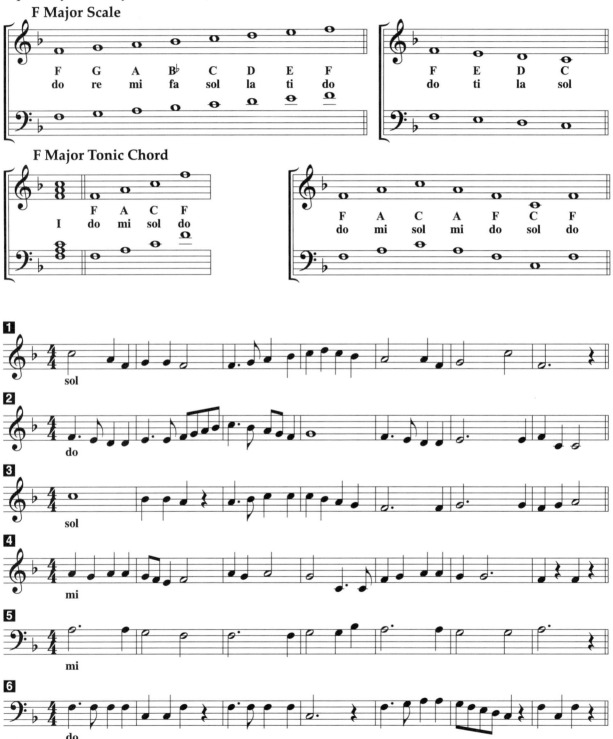

# Practice

◆ Pitch and Rhythm • Dotted Notes in $\frac{3}{4}$ Meter

Using the F major patterns below as a guide, sight-sing the following exercises separately or in any combination.

# Wake Up

Words and Music by
EMILY CROCKER

# Pitch

## ◆ The D Minor Scale

The minor scale is a specific arrangement of whole steps and half steps:

$$W \; + \; H \; + \; W \; + \; W \; + \; H \; + \; W \; + \; W$$

The D minor scale is a minor scale that starts and ends on D. To build this scale, begin on D and use the pattern of whole steps and half steps shown above. Notice the need for a B♭. Play the D minor scale on the piano.

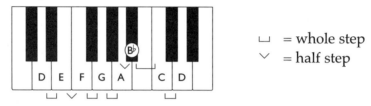

⌣ = whole step
⌄ = half step

Sing the D minor scale using solfège syllables. Where do the whole steps occur? Where do the half steps occur?

The D minor scale is called the relative minor of the F major scale, since both scales have the same half steps (E and F, *ti* and *do*; A and B♭, *mi* and *fa*).

## ◆ Key Signature

In the key of D minor, there will always be a B♭.
The key signature for D minor looks like this:

## ◆ Practice

Sight-sing the following exercise that uses pitches found in the D minor scale.

# Practice

◆ Pitch and Rhythm • D Minor in $\frac{3}{4}$ and $\frac{4}{4}$ Meter

Using the D minor patterns below as a guide, sight-sing the following sets of exercises separately or in any combination.

# A Wish

Words and Music by
AUDREY SNYDER

# Evaluation

Demonstrate what you have learned in Chapter Four by completing the following:

◆ **Musical Math**

When the quarter notes receives the beat:

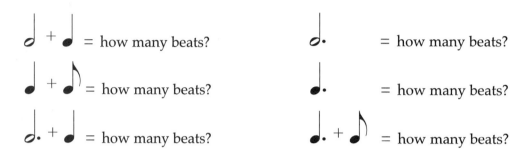

♩ + ♩ = how many beats?          ♩. = how many beats?

♩ + ♪ = how many beats?          ♩. = how many beats?

♩. + ♩ = how many beats?          ♩. + ♪ = how many beats?

◆ Clap, tap or chant the following exercises.

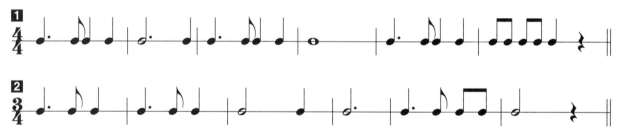

◆ Sight-sing the following exercise.

◆ Sight-sing the following melody.

Theme excerpt from "The New World Symphony"                    Dvořák

# CHAPTER 5

# Rhythm

## ◆ Sixteenth Notes

The **beat** is *the steady pulse of all music.* **Rhythm** is *the combination of long and short notes and rests.*

A **sixteenth note** is *a note that represents one quarter beat of sound when the quarter note receives the beat.* Four sixteenth notes equal one beat of sound when the quarter note receives the beat.

Sixteenth Notes

## ◆ Practice

Clap, tap or chant the following exercises to practice reading sixteenth notes.

# Rhythm

## ◆ Sixteenth and Eighth Note Combinations

A **sixteenth note** is *a note that represents one quarter beat of sound when the quarter note receives the beat.* Four sixteenth notes equal one beat of sound when the quarter note receives the beat. Sixteenth notes can be combined with a variety of notes. Often, sixteenth notes are combined with eighth notes.

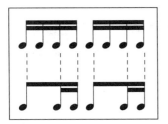

Note Combinations

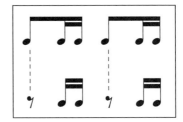

Note and Rest Combinations

## ◆ Practice

Clap, tap or chant while conducting the following exercises to practice reading sixteenth and eighth note combinations. Keep the beat steady.

# Rhythm

## ◆ More Sixteenth and Eighth Note Combinations

Sixteenth notes can be combined with a variety of notes. Often, sixteenth notes are combined with eighth notes.

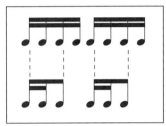

Note Combinations

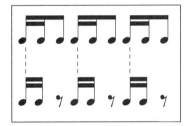

Note and Rest Combinations

## ◆ Practice

Clap, tap or chant while conducting the following exercises to practice reading sixteenth and eighth note combinations.

# Crazy Calendar

Words from an anonymous text
Adapted by AUDREY SNYDER

Music by
AUDREY SNYDER

# Rhythm

◆ **Time Signature • $\frac{2}{4}$ Meter**

$\frac{2}{4}$ **meter** is *a time signature in which there are two beats per measure and the quarter note receives the beat*. A whole rest ▬ in $\frac{2}{4}$ meter represents one measure of silence.

$$\mathbf{2} = \text{two beats per measure}$$
$$\mathbf{4} = \text{the quarter note receives the beat}$$

Study and practice the conducting pattern to the right.

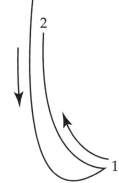

◆ **Practice**

Chant the rhythms in the following exercises as you conduct.

# Pasta Plus

Words and Music by
AUDREY SNYDER

# Practice

◆ Pitch and Rhythm • D Minor in $\frac{2}{4}$ Meter

Using the D minor patterns below as a guide, sight-sing the following exercises separately or in any combination.

# Cool

Words and Music by
EMILY CROCKER

Rhythmic (♩ = 88)

Piano

*mf*

**5**

Part I *mf*

1. Shei - la was a danc - er, quite ac - com - plished at Ma - dame Bil - lie's Tap and
2. Le - o was an art - ist from the time that he could hold a cray - on

Part II *mf*

1. Shei - la was a danc - er, quite ac - com - plished at Ma - dame Bil - lie's Tap and
2. Le - o was an art - ist from the time that he could hold a cray - on

Bal - let School, per - fect - ing all the com - plex com - bi - na - tions,
in his hand. Now he en - ters all the com - pe - ti - tions,

Bal - let School, per - fect - ing all the com - plex com - bi - na - tions,
in his hand. Now he en - ters all the com - pe - ti - tions,

# Pitch

## ◆ The C Major Tonic and Dominant Chords

A **chord** is *the combination of three or more notes played or sung at the same time.* The **tonic chord** is *a chord built on the home tone, or keynote, of a scale.* In a major scale, this chord uses the notes *do, mi* and *sol* and is sometimes called the **I** ("one") chord, since it is based on the first note of the scale, or *do.*

Chords can be built on any note of the scale. The **dominant chord** is *a chord built on the fifth note of a scale.* In a major scale, this chord uses the notes *sol, ti* and *re* and is sometimes called the **V** ("five") chord, since it is based on the fifth note of the scale, or *sol.*

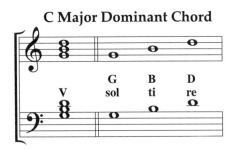

## ◆ Practice

Sight-sing, separately or in any combination, the following exercises that use pitches found in the C major tonic and dominant chords.

# Practice

◆ **Pitch and Rhythm • C Major Tonic and Dominant Chords**

Using the C major patterns below as a guide, sight-sing the following exercises separately or in any combination.

# Pitch

## ◆ More About Minor

A **minor scale** is *a scale that has* la *as its home tone, or keynote*. It is made up of a specific arrangement of whole steps and half steps in the following order:  W  +  H  +  W  +  W  +  H  +  W  +  W.

Sometimes, altered pitches are used in minor keys. A **sharp** (♯) is *a symbol that raises the pitch of a given note one half step*. A **flat** (♭) is *a symbol that lowers the pitch of a given note one half step*. A **natural** (♮) is *a symbol that cancels a previous sharp or flat, or a sharp or flat in a key signature*. An **accidental** (another name for an altered pitch) is *any sharp, flat or natural that is not included in the key signature of a piece of music*.

## ◆ The Natural Minor Scale

The **natural minor scale** is *a minor scale that uses no altered pitches or accidentals*. Play the A natural minor scale on the piano, and sing the scale using solfège syllables.

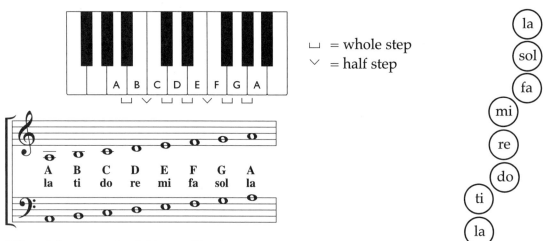

## ◆ The Harmonic Minor Scale

The **harmonic minor scale** is *a minor scale that uses a raised seventh note*, si *(raised from* sol*)*. The seventh note is also known as the leading tone, since it creates a strong feeling of motion toward the tonic, or *la*. Play the A harmonic minor scale on the piano, and sing the scale using solfège syllables.

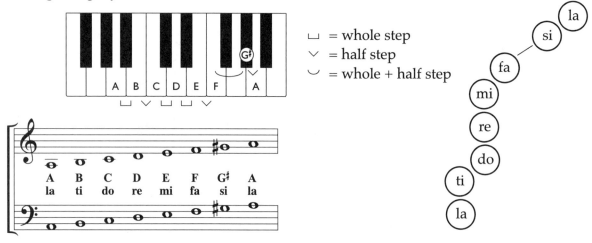

## ◆ The Melodic Minor Scale

The **melodic minor scale** is *a minor scale that uses raised sixth and seventh notes,* fi *(raised from* fa*) and* si *(raised from* sol*).* Often, these notes are raised in ascending patterns, but not in descending patterns. Play the A melodic minor scale on the piano, and sing the scale using solfège syllables.

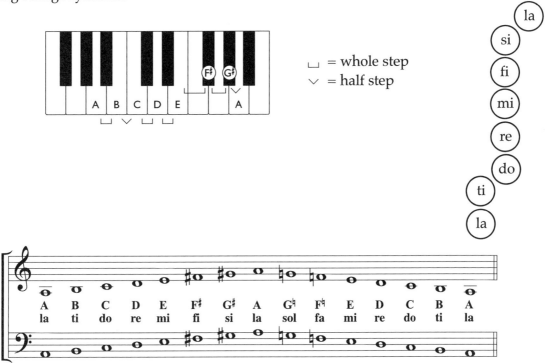

⌣ = whole step
∨ = half step

## ◆ Practice

Sight-sing the following exercises that use altered pitches or accidentals.

*\* An altered pitch continues through the measure unless cancelled.*

# Pitch

## ◆ The A Minor Tonic and Dominant Chords

A **chord** is *the combination of three or more notes played or sung at the same time.* The **tonic chord** is *a chord built on the home tone, or keynote, of a scale.* In a minor scale, this chord uses the notes *la, do* and *mi* and is sometimes called the **i** ("one") chord, since it is based on the first note of the scale, or *la.*

A Minor Tonic Chord

The **dominant chord** is *a chord built on the fifth note of a scale.* In a minor scale, this chord uses the notes *mi, sol* and *ti* (or *mi, si* and *ti*) and is sometimes called the **v** or **V** ("five") chord, since it is based on the fifth note of the scale, or *mi.*

A Minor
Dominant Chord

A Minor
Dominant Chord (raised 7th)

## ◆ Practice

Sight-sing, separately or in any combination, the following exercises that use pitches found in the A minor tonic and dominant chords.

# Practice

◆ Pitch and Rhythm • A Minor Tonic and Dominant Chords

Using the A minor patterns below as a guide, and adjusting to fit your vocal range, sight-sing the following exercises.

# Remember

Words and Music by
EMILY CROCKER

*Second time observe fermata

# Evaluation

Demonstrate what you have learned in Chapter Five by completing the following:

## ◆ Reviewing Rhythm and Chords

1. When the quarter note receives the beat, how many sixteenth notes are there per beat?
2. What kind of major chord is built on the keynote of the scale (or *do*)?
3. What kind of major chord is built on the fifth note of the scale (or *sol*)?

◆ Sight-sing the following melodies.

◆ Name the notes in the following chords and sing them using solfège syllables.

**C Major Tonic Chord**

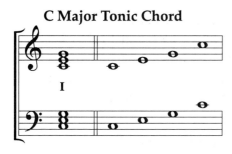

I

**A Minor Tonic Chord**

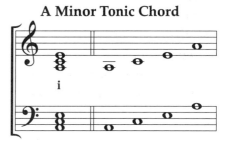

i

**C Major Dominant Chord**

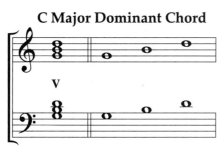

V

**A Minor
Dominant Chord (raised 7th)**

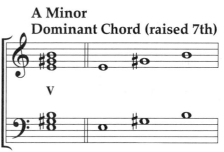

V

◆ Sight-sing the following melody.

Le Roi Petite

la

## ◆ Be A Composer

Copy the following set of measures on a sheet of paper. Use the rhythms given to create your own musical pattern. Add pitches and transfer your pattern to a staff.

# CHAPTER 6

# Pitch

## ◆ The F Major Tonic and Dominant Chords

The **tonic chord** is *a chord built on the home tone, or keynote, of a scale.* In a major scale, this chord uses the notes *do, mi* and *sol* and is sometimes called the **I** ("one") chord, since it is based on the first note of the scale, or *do.* The **dominant chord** is *a chord built on the fifth note of a scale.* In a major scale, this chord uses the notes *sol, ti* and *re* and is sometimes called the **V** ("five") chord, since it is based on the fifth note of the scale, or *sol.*

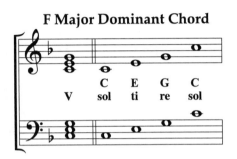

## ◆ Practice

Read and echo the following exercises to practice singing intervals found in the F major tonic and dominant chords. Which exercises use the tonic chords? Which exercises use the dominant chords?

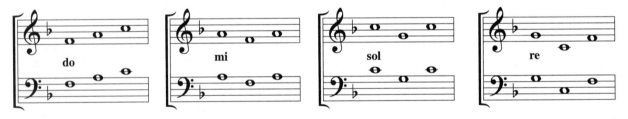

Sight-sing the following exercises that use pitches found in the F major tonic and dominant chords.

# Practice

## ◆ Pitch and Rhythm • F Major Tonic and Dominant Chords

Using the F major patterns below as a guide, sight-sing the following exercises separately or in any combination.

# Pitch

## ◆ The D Minor Tonic and Dominant Chords

The **tonic chord** is *a chord built on the home tone, or keynote, of a scale.* In a minor scale, this chord uses the notes *la, do* and *mi* and is sometimes called the **i** ("one") chord, since it is based on the first note of the scale, or *la.*

The **dominant chord** is *a chord built on the fifth note of a scale.* In a minor scale, this chord uses the notes *mi, sol* and *ti* (or *mi, si* and *ti*) and is sometimes called the **v** or **V** ("five") chord, since it is based on the fifth note of the scale, or *mi.*

## ◆ Practice

Read and echo the following exercises to practice singing intervals found in the D minor tonic and dominant chords.

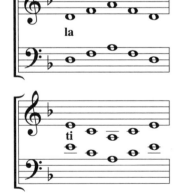

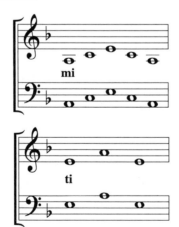

# Practice

## ◆ Pitch and Rhythm • D Minor Tonic and Dominant Chords

Using the D minor patterns below as a guide, sight-sing the following exercises separately or in any combination.

When singing this song, notice that it is in the key of F major. However, there is a section in the middle that is in the key of D minor. In which measure does the D minor tonality start? In which measure does it return to F major?

# Fish Story

Words and Music by
AUDREY SNYDER

# Pitch

## ◆ The G Major Scale

A **sharp** is *a symbol that raises the pitch of a given note one half step.* The note to the right, F♯ (F sharp), is written with the sharp sign to the left of the notehead.

The major scale is a specific arrangement of whole steps and half steps: W + W + H + W + W + W + H.

The G major scale is a major scale that starts and ends on G. To build this scale, begin on G and use the pattern of whole steps and half steps shown above. Notice the need for an F♯. Play the G major scale on the piano.

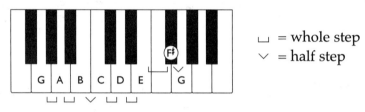

⌴ = whole step
∨ = half step

Sing the G major scale using solfège syllables. Where do the whole steps occur? Where do the half steps occur?

## ◆ Key Signature

In the key of G major, there will always be an F♯. The key signature for G major looks like this:

## ◆ Practice

Read and echo the following exercises to practice singing notes from the G major scale.

# Pitch

### ◆ The G Major Tonic and Dominant Chords

The **tonic chord** is *a chord built on the home tone, or keynote, of a scale.* The **dominant chord** is *a chord built on the fifth note of a scale.*

### ◆ Practice

Read and echo the following examples to practice intervals found in the G major tonic chord.

Read and echo the following examples to practice intervals found in the G major dominant chord.

# Practice

## ◆ Pitch and Rhythm • G Major Tonic and Dominant Chords

Using the G major patterns below as a guide, sight-sing the following sets of exercises separately or in any combination.

# By The Fireside

Words and Music by
AUDREY SNYDER

snow.

snow. Here, by the fire-side, in the flick-'ring fire-light, flames are burn-ing bright.

snow. Here, by the fire - side, flames are burn-ing bright.

Though it may storm and rage out - side, we're safe and warm to - night. So

Though it may storm and rage out - side, we're safe and warm to - night.

Though it may storm and rage out - side, we're safe and warm to - night.

# Evaluation

Demonstrate what you have learned in Chapter Six by completing the following:

◆ In the key of D minor:
1. What is the letter name of the tonic note? What is its solfège syllable?
2. What is the letter name of the dominant note? What is its solfège syllable?

◆ In the key of G major:
1. What is the letter name of the tonic note? What is its solfège syllable?
2. What is the letter name of the dominant note? What is its solfège syllable?

## Musical Math

The rhythm ♪♪♪♪ equals the same amount of time as how many eighth notes?

The rhythm ♩♪♪ equals the same amount of time as how many quarter notes?

## True or False?

The following rhythms ‿♪♪ and ♪♪♪ equal the same amount of time.

◆ Sight-sing the following exercises. Which exercises are in G major? Which are in D minor?

# CHAPTER 7

# Rhythm

### ◆ Dotted Eighth and Sixteenth Note Combinations

Dotted rhythms are often combinations of unequal note values. The rhythmic pattern to the right uses dotted eighth notes followed by sixteenth notes. This rhythm is a "long-short" pattern.

Another combination is the sixteenth note followed by a dotted eighth note, as shown to the right. This rhythm is a "short-long" pattern.

### ◆ Practice

Clap, tap or chant while conducting the following exercises that use dotted eighth and sixteenth note combinations.

# Practice

### ◆ Pitch and Rhythm • Dotted Eighth and Sixteenth Notes in G Major

Using the G major patterns below as a guide, sight-sing the following exercises separately or in any combination.

# Pitch

## ◆ The E Minor Scale

The minor scale is a specific arrangement of whole steps and half steps:

$$W + H + W + W + H + W + W$$

The E minor scale is a minor scale that starts and ends on E. To build this scale, begin on E and use the pattern of whole steps and half steps shown above. Notice the need for an F♯. Play the E minor scale on the piano.

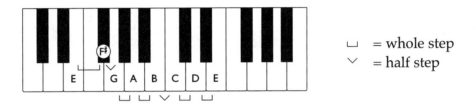

⌐ = whole step
∨ = half step

Sing the E minor scale using solfège syllables. Where do the whole steps occur? Where do the half steps occur?

The E minor scale is called the relative minor of the G major scale, since both scales have the same half steps (F♯ and G, *ti* and *do*; B and C, *mi* and *fa*).

## ◆ Key Signature

In the key of E minor, there will always be an F♯. The key signature for E minor looks like this:

## ◆ Practice

Sight-sing the following exercise to practice singing notes from the E minor scale.

# Pitch

### ◆ The E Minor Tonic and Dominant Chords

The **tonic chord** is *a chord built on the home tone, or keynote, of a scale.* The **dominant chord** is *a chord built on the fifth note of a scale.*

### ◆ Practice

Read and echo the following exercises to practice singing intervals found in the E minor tonic and dominant chords.

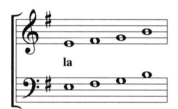

Sight-sing the following exercises that use pitches found in the E minor tonic and dominant chords.

# Practice

## ◆ Pitch and Rhythm • E Minor Tonic and Dominant Chords

Using the E minor patterns below as a guide, sight-sing the following exercises separately or in any combination.

# Danza!

Words and Music by
EMILY CROCKER

With vigor (♩ = 116)

Play tam - bou - rine and dance in a ring,

Play tam - bou - rine and dance in a ring,

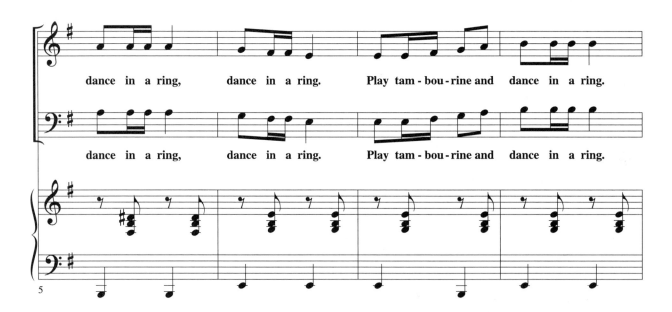

dance in a ring,     dance in a ring.     Play tam - bou - rine and     dance in a ring.

dance in a ring,     dance in a ring.     Play tam - bou - rine and     dance in a ring.

dance in a ring, dance in a ring, dance in a ring.

dance in a ring, dance in a ring, dance in a ring.

Play tam-bou-rine and dance in a ring. Dance in a ring to-geth - er.

Play tam-bou-rine and dance in a ring. Dance in a ring to-geth - er.

Dan - za, dan - za, dan - za!

Dan - za, dan - za, dan - za.

# Rhythm

## ◆ Mixed Meter

**Mixed meter** is *a technique in which the time signature or meter changes frequently within a piece of music.*

In $\frac{2}{4}$, $\frac{3}{4}$ and $\frac{4}{4}$ meters, the quarter note beat remains the same, but the number of beats per measure changes.

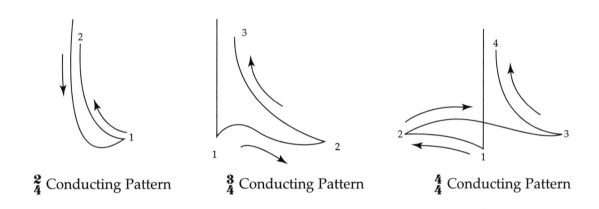

$\frac{2}{4}$ Conducting Pattern          $\frac{3}{4}$ Conducting Pattern          $\frac{4}{4}$ Conducting Pattern

## ◆ Practice

Using the conducting patterns above as a guide, chant the rhythms in the following exercise. Keep the beat steady.

# Rhythm

### ◆ Swing Rhythms

In many jazz, blues and pop styles of music, swing rhythms are often used. **Swing rhythms** are *rhythms in which the second eighth note of each beat is played or sung like the last third of a triplet.* To learn more about triplets, see page 135.

Dotted patterns are also common in swing rhythms and are played or sung like triplets.

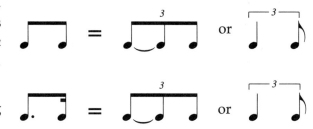

To learn more about triplets, see page 135.

## SIGHT-SING

In this song, speak the dotted rhythms in a swing style.

# Match Cats, Cool Cats Redux

**Words and Music by
EMILY CROCKER**

# Pitch

## ◆ The D Major Scale

The major scale is a specific arrangement of whole steps and half steps:

$$W + W + H + W + W + W + H$$

The D major scale is a major scale that starts and ends on D. To build this scale, begin on D and use the pattern of whole steps and half steps shown above. Notice the need for an F♯ and C♯. Play the D major scale on the piano.

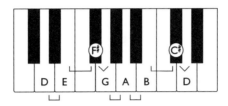

⌐ = whole step
∨ = half step

Sing the D major scale using solfège syllables. Where do the whole steps occur? Where do the half steps occur?

## ◆ Key Signature

In the key of D major, there will always be an F♯ and C♯. The key signature for D major looks like this:

## ◆ Practice

Read and echo the following examples to practice singing notes from the D major scale.

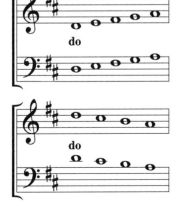

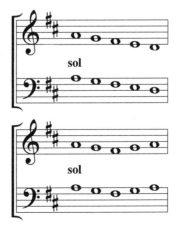

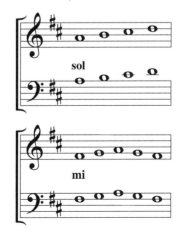

# Pitch

## ◆ The D Major Tonic and Dominant Chords

The **tonic chord** is *a chord built on the home tone, or keynote, of a scale.* The **dominant chord** is *a chord built on the fifth note of a scale.*

## ◆ Practice

Read and echo the following exercises to practice singing intervals found in the D major tonic and dominant chords.

 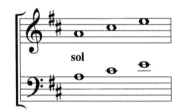 

Sight-sing the following exercises that use pitches found in the D major tonic and dominant chords.

# Practice

◆ Pitch and Rhythm • D Major Tonic and Dominant Chords

Using the D major patterns below as a guide, sight-sing the following exercises separately or in any combination.

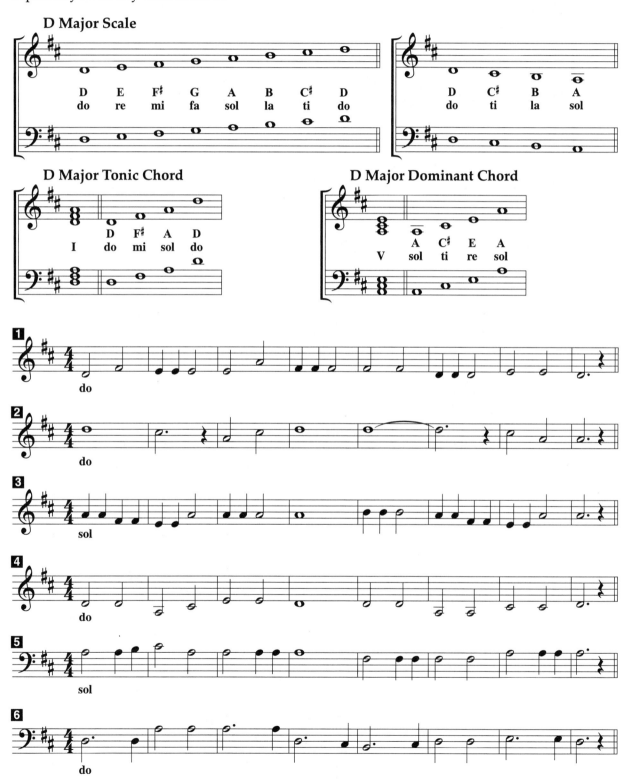

# The Evening Sun

Words by EMILY BRONTË
(1818 - 1848)

Music by AUDREY SNYDER

felt the sooth - ing breeze. The eve - ning

felt the sooth - ing breeze. Ah.

felt the sooth - ing breeze. Ah.

sun was sink - ing down.

*rit.*

# Pitch

## ◆ The B Minor Scale

The minor scale is a specific arrangement of whole steps and half steps:

$$W \; + \; H \; + \; W \; + \; W \; + \; H \; + \; W \; + \; W$$

The B minor scale is a minor scale that starts and ends on B. To build this scale, begin on B and use the pattern of whole steps and half steps shown above. Notice the need for an F♯ and C♯. Play the B minor scale on the piano.

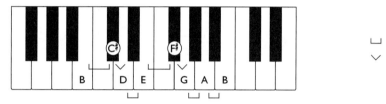

⌐⌐ = whole step
⌄ = half step

Sing the B minor scale using solfège syllables. Where do the whole steps occur? Where do the half steps occur?

The B minor scale is called the relative minor of the D major scale, since both scales have the same half steps (C♯ and D, *ti* and *do;* F♯ and G, *mi* and *fa*).

## ◆ Key Signature

In the key of B minor, there will always be an F♯ and C♯. The key signature for B minor looks like this:

## ◆ Practice

Read and echo the following examples to practice singing notes from the B minor scale.

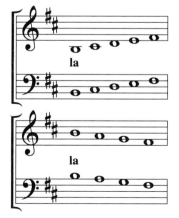

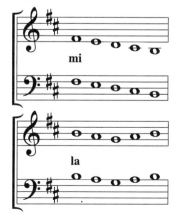

# Pitch

## ◆ The B Minor Tonic and Dominant Chords

The **tonic chord** is *a chord built on the home tone, or keynote, of a scale.* The **dominant chord** is *a chord built on the fifth note of a scale.*

## ◆ Practice

Read and echo the following exercises to practice singing intervals found in the B minor tonic and dominant chords.

Sight-sing the following exercises that use pitches found in the B minor tonic and dominant chords.

# Practice

◆ Pitch and Rhythm • B Minor Tonic and Dominant Chords

Using the B minor patterns below as a guide, sight-sing the following exercises separately or in any combination.

# Evaluation

Demonstrate what you have learned in Chapter Seven by completing the following:

## ◆ Which Rhythm?

With a partner, take turns clapping the patterns below. Identify which pattern your partner is clapping.

## ◆ Write-A-Rhythm

When the quarter note receives the beat, each of the following rhythm patterns receive one beat.

Copy the following measures on a piece of paper. Using the rhythms above, fill in each measure to equal two beats. Clap your composition, and trade with your partner. Finally, clap your partner's composition.

## ◆ Which Meter?

In the exercise below, count the number of beats in each measure and identify each meter. Then, clap, tap or chant while conducting the rhythms. Keep the beat steady.

◆ Match the following scales to the correct label:

B melodic minor    B natural minor        D major            E melodic minor

E natural minor                    G major

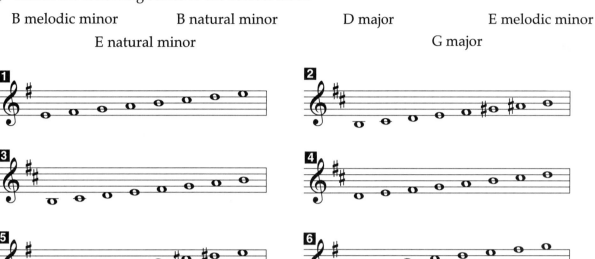

◆ Sight-sing the following melodies.

# CHAPTER 8

# Pitch

## ◆ The C Major Tonic, Dominant and Subdominant Chords

The **tonic chord** is *a chord built on the home tone, or keynote, of a scale.* The **dominant chord** is *a chord built on the fifth note of a scale.*

C Major
Tonic Chord

C Major
Dominant Chord

The **subdominant chord** is *a chord built on the fourth note of a scale.* In a major scale, this chord uses the notes *fa, la* and *do,* and is sometimes called the **IV** ("four") chord, since it is based on the fourth note of the scale, or *fa.*

C Major
Subdominant Chord

## ◆ Practice

Sight-sing the following exercises that use pitches found in the C major tonic, dominant and subdominant chords.

# Practice

◆ Pitch and Rhythm • C Major Tonic, Dominant and Subdominant Chords

Using the C major patterns below as a guide, sight-sing the following exercises separately or in any combination.

# Pitch

## ◆ The F Major Tonic, Dominant and Subdominant Chords

The **tonic chord** is *a chord built on the home tone, or keynote, of a scale.* The **dominant chord** is *a chord built on the fifth note of a scale.*

The **subdominant chord** is *a chord built on the fourth note of a scale.*

## ◆ Practice

Sight-sing the following exercises that use pitches found in the F major tonic, dominant and subdominant chords.

# Rhythm

## ◆ Simple Meter and Compound Meter

The **beat** is *the steady pulse of all music.* **Simple meter** is *any meter in which the quarter note receives the beat, and the division of the beat is based on two eighth notes.* $\frac{2}{4}$, $\frac{3}{4}$ and $\frac{4}{4}$ meters are examples of simple meter.

**2** = two beats per measure
**4** = the quarter note receives the beat

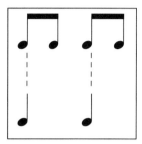

**Compound meter** is *any meter in which the dotted quarter note receives the beat, and the division of the beat is based on three eighth notes.* $\frac{6}{8}$ meter is an example of compound meter.

**6** = two groups of three eighth notes per measure
**8** = the dotted quarter note receives the beat

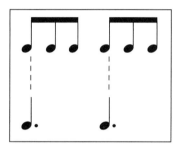

Like $\frac{2}{4}$, $\frac{6}{8}$ meter is usually conducted in two (except when the tempo is very slow).

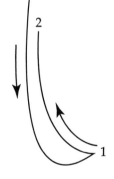

## ◆ Practice

Chant the rhythms of the following exercises as you conduct.

# Rhythm

## ◆ Time Signature • $\frac{6}{8}$ Meter

**Compound meter** is *any meter in which the dotted quarter note receives the beat, and the division of the beat is based on three eighth notes.* $\frac{6}{8}$ meter is an example of compound meter. The following rhythms are all common in $\frac{6}{8}$ meter.

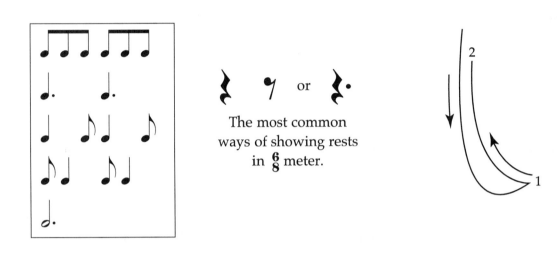

The most common ways of showing rests in $\frac{6}{8}$ meter.

## ◆ Practice

$\frac{6}{8}$ meter is usually conducted in two, unless the tempo is very slow. Clap, tap or chant while conducting the following exercises to practice reading rhythms in $\frac{6}{8}$ meter.

# Practice

◆ Pitch and Rhythm • F Major in $\frac{6}{8}$ Meter

Using the F major patterns below as a guide, sight-sing the following exercises separately or in any combination.

# Sing With Joy This Morning

German Carol

Arranged with new lyrics by
EMILY CROCKER

le - lu - ia,  for  joy  is  our  this  morn - ing. _____

le - lu - ia,  for  joy  is  our  this  morn - ing. _____

le,  al - le - lu - ia,  this  morn - ing. _____

Sing  with  joy _____  this  morn - ing. _____

Sing _ with  joy _____  this  morn - ing. _____

Sing  with  joy _____  this  morn - ing. _____

# Evaluation

Demonstrate what you have learned in Chapter Eight by completing the following:

◆ Name the notes in the following chords, and sing them using solfège syllables.

◆ Sight-sing the following melodies.

# Evaluation

◆ ## Simple or Compound Meter?

Which of the following phrases best describes simple meter? Which best describes compound meter?

1. A meter in which the division of the beat is based on two eighth notes.
2. A meter in which the division of the beat is based on three eighth notes.
3. $\frac{2}{4}$, $\frac{3}{4}$ or $\frac{4}{4}$ meter.
4. $\frac{6}{8}$ meter.
5. A meter in which the quarter note receives the beat.
6. A meter in which the dotted quarter note receives the beat.

◆ Sight-sing the following melody.

Shooting The Rapids

do

◆ ## Be A Composer

Each of the following rhythms equals one measure in $\frac{6}{8}$ meter. Create your own rhythm composition by combining and repeating these rhythms in any order you choose. For an extra challenge, add percussion instruments or create a melody based on your rhythms.

# Pitch

## ◆ The B♭ Major Scale

The major scale is a specific arrangement of whole steps and half steps:

$$W + W + H + W + W + W + H$$

The B♭ major scale is a major scale that starts and ends on B♭. To build this scale, begin on B♭ and use the pattern of whole steps and half steps shown above. Notice the need for a B♭ and E♭. Play the B♭ major scale on the piano.

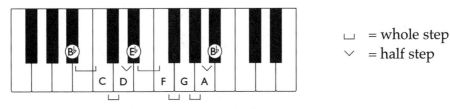

⌐⌐ = whole step
∨ = half step

Sing the B♭ major scale using solfège syllables. Where do the whole steps occur? Where do the half steps occur?

## ◆ Key Signature

In the key of B♭ major, there will always be a B♭ and E♭. The key signature for B♭ major looks like this:

## ◆ Practice

Read and echo the following exercises to practice singing notes from the B♭ major scale.

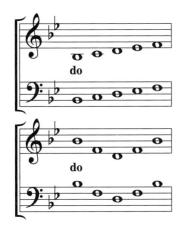

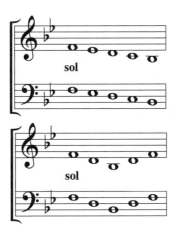

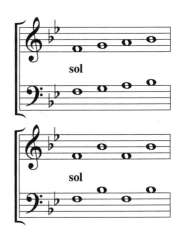

# Pitch

### ◆ The B♭ Major Tonic, Dominant and Subdominant Chords

The **tonic chord** is *a chord built on the home tone, or keynote, of a scale.* The **dominant chord** is *a chord built on the fifth note of a scale.*

The **subdominant chord** is *a chord built on the fourth note of a scale.*

### ◆ Practice

Sight-sing the following exercises that use pitches found in the B♭ major tonic, dominant and subdominant chords.

# Practice

◆ Pitch and Rhythm • B♭ Major Tonic, Dominant and Subdominant Chords

Using the B♭ major patterns below as a guide, sight-sing the following exercises separately or in any combination.

# Ancient Battlefield

Words and Music by
AUDREY SNYDER

# Terms and Symbols

## ◆ Accent >

An **accent** is *a symbol placed above or below a given note that indicates the note should receive extra emphasis or stress.*

Accented Notes

In order to establish the feel of the meter, it is important to stress the first beat of the measure. Sight-sing the following exercise, placing stress on the accented notes.

**1**

## ◆ Syncopation

**Syncopation** *occurs when the accent is placed on notes that normally do not receive extra emphasis.* Syncopation is common in pop, rock, jazz and classical music.

## ◆ Practice

Read and echo the following examples to practice rhythms with syncopation.

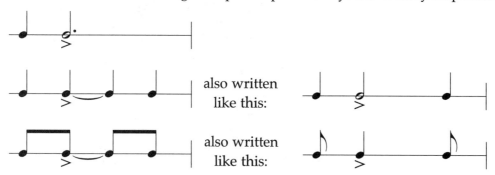

also written like this:

Clap, tap or chant while conducting the following exercises to practice reading rhythms with syncopation.

**2**

**3**

**4**

**5**

# Practice

◆ Rhythm • Syncopation
Read and echo the following exercises to practice common rhythms with syncopation.

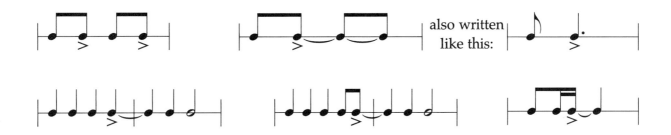

Clap, tap or chant while conducting the following exercises to practice reading rhythms with syncopation.

# Practice

### ◆ Pitch and Rhythm • Syncopation in B♭ Major

Using the B♭ major patterns below as a guide, sight-sing the following exercises separately or in any combination. After the first measure of each exercise, continue to emphasize the syncopated notes, even though the accents are not marked in the music.

# Talk To Me

Words and Music by
**AUDREY SNYDER**

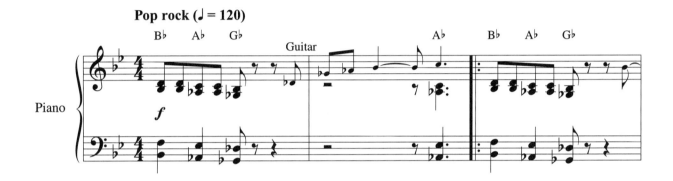

*Pronounce the words in a rock or pop style, e.g. "Never ged-n-answer."

# Evaluation

Demonstrate what you have learned in Chapter Nine by completing the following:

◆ In major keys:
 1. Tonic chords use which three solfège syllables?
 2. Dominant chords use which three solfège syllables?
 3. Subdominant chords use which three solfège syllables?

◆ Sight-sing the following exercise.

◆ Answer the following questions:
 1. What symbol > is this?
 2. When accents are placed on notes that normally do not receive extra emphasis, what is it called?

◆ Sight-sing the following exercise.

# CHAPTER 10

# Pitch

### ◆ The G Minor Scale

The minor scale is a specific arrangement of whole steps and half steps:

$$W + H + W + W + H + W + W$$

The G minor scale is a minor scale that starts and ends on G. To build this scale, begin on G and use the pattern of whole steps and half steps shown above. Notice the need for a B♭ and E♭. Play the G minor scale on the piano.

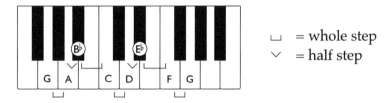

⌣ = whole step
∨ = half step

Sing the G minor scale using solfège syllables. Where do the whole steps occur? Where do the half steps occur?

The G minor scale is called the relative minor of the B♭ major scale, since both scales have the same half steps (A and B♭, *ti* and *do*; D and E♭, *mi* and *fa*).

### ◆ Key Signature

In the key of G minor, there will always be a B♭ and E♭. The key signature for G minor looks like this:

### ◆ The G Minor Tonic, Dominant and Subdominant Chords

The **tonic chord** is *a chord built on the home tone, or keynote, of a scale.* The **dominant chord** is *a chord built on the fifth note of a scale.* The **subdominant chord** is *a chord built on the fourth note of a scale.*

# Practice

## ◆ Pitch and Rhythm • G Minor Tonic, Dominant and Subdominant Chords

Using the G minor patterns below as a guide, sight-sing the following exercises separately or in any combination.

# Rhythm

## ◆ Borrowed Division • Triplets and Duplets

The **beat** is *the steady pulse of all music.*

**Simple meter** is *any meter in which the quarter note receives the beat, and the division of the beat is based on two eighth notes.* $\frac{2}{4}$, $\frac{3}{4}$ and $\frac{4}{4}$ meters are examples of simple meter.

**Compound meter** is *any meter in which the dotted quarter note receives the beat, and the division of the beat is based on three eighth notes.* $\frac{6}{8}$ is an example of compound meter.

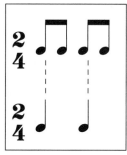

Simple Meter

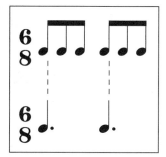

Compound Meter

Sometimes in simple meter it is necessary for the beat to be divided into three. Likewise, in compound meter, it is sometimes necessary for the beat to divided into two. When this happens, it is known as the borrowed division of the beat .

In simple meter, the borrowed division is called a triplet, since it is a division of three where two would normally be. In compound meter, the borrowed division is called a duplet, since it is a division of two where three would normally be.

Look at the following examples and notice how these are notated with a bracket over the borrowed grouping of notes. In some cases, there is only a number and no bracket.

## ◆ Practice

Clap, tap or chant while conducting the following exercises to practice reading triplets and duplets. Keep the beat steady.

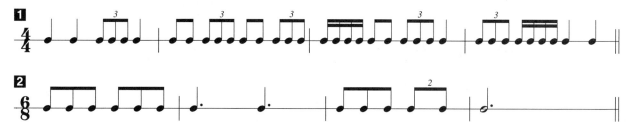

# Tell Me, Why Do You Sigh?

Words and Music by
EMILY CROCKER

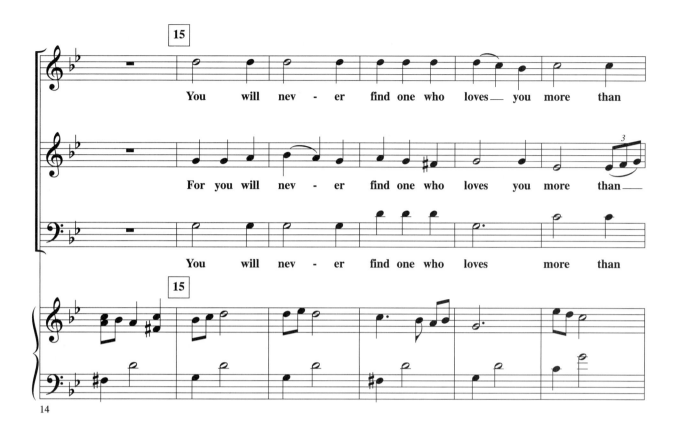

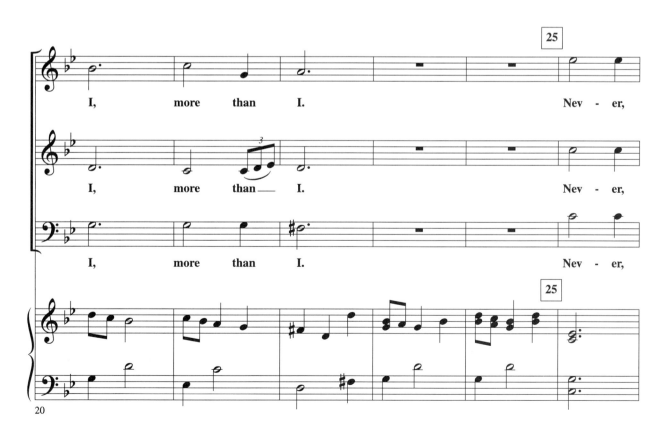

never, nev - er find one who loves you more _____ than

nev - er, nev - er _____ find one who loves you more _____ than

nev - er, nev - er find one who loves you more _____ than

26

34

I. Oo, _____ Oo. _____

I. Oo, _____ Oo. _____

I. Oo, _____ Oo. _____

34

33

# Rhythm

## ◆ More Simple Meters

**Meter** is *a way of organizing rhythm*. Meter, also called time signature, groups a specific number of beats per measure and assigns a particular note value to receive the beat.

**4** = four beats per measure          **3** = three beats per measure
**4** = the quarter note receives the beat          **4** = the quarter note receives the beat

**Simple meter** is *any meter in which the quarter note receives the beat and the division of the beat is based on two eighth notes*. However, other note values can receive the beat in simple meter, such as the eighth note and half note.

**3** = three beats per measure          **3** = three beats per measure
**2** = the half note receives the beat          **8** = the eighth note receives the beat

Music can be grouped according to the beat, or the division or subdivision of the beat. Clap, tap or chant the rhythms in the exercises below. Notice a new rhythmic value in the **3/8** example. The notes with three beams are called 32nd notes and are created by subdividing the sixteenth notes.

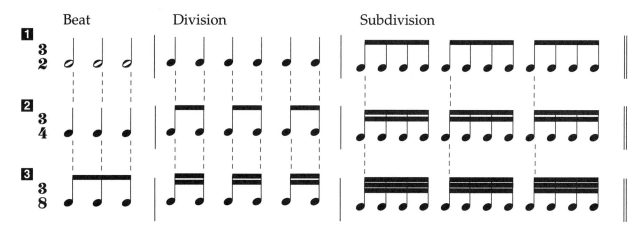

## ◆ Practice

Clap, tap or chant while conducting the following exercise. Keep the beat steady as indicated between the **3/4**, **3/2** and **3/8** meters.

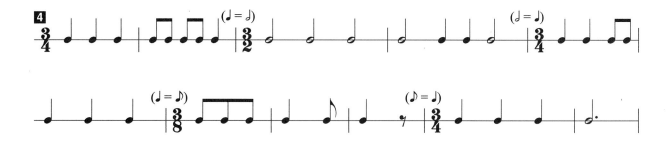

# Rhythm

◆ Time Signature • $\frac{2}{2}$ Meter and Cut Time • ¢

**Cut time** is *another name for* $\frac{2}{2}$ *meter*. In both meters, there are two beats per measure and the half note receives the beat.

◆ Practice

Clap, tap or chant while conducting the following exercises to practice reading rhythmic patterns in cut time.

**1**

**2**

Sight-sing the following exercise in $\frac{2}{2}$ meter.

**3**

la

◆ Challenge

Conduct in two while you sing.

# Pitch

### ◆ The E♭ Major Scale

The major scale is a specific arrangement of whole steps and half steps:

W + W + H + W + W + W + H

The E♭ major scale is a major scale that starts and ends on E♭. To build this scale, begin on E♭ and use the pattern of whole steps and half steps shown above. Notice the need for a B♭, E♭ and A♭. Play the E♭ major scale on the piano.

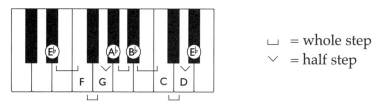

⌐ = whole step
∨ = half step

Sing the E♭ major scale using solfège syllables. Where do the whole steps occur? Where do the half steps occur?

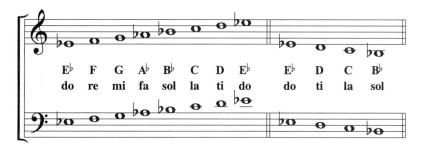

| E♭ | F | G | A♭ | B♭ | C | D | E♭ | | E♭ | D | C | B♭ |
|----|---|---|----|----|---|---|----|--|----|---|---|----|
| do | re | mi | fa | sol | la | ti | do | | do | ti | la | sol |

### ◆ Key Signature

In the key of E♭ major, there will always be a B♭, E♭ and A♭. The key signature for E♭ major looks like this:

### ◆ The E♭ Major Tonic, Dominant and Subdominant Chords

The **tonic chord** is *a chord built on the home tone, or keynote, of a scale.* The **dominant chord** is *a chord built on the fifth note of a scale.* The **subdominant chord** is *a chord built on the fourth note of a scale.*

**E♭ Major Tonic Chord**

| | E♭ | G | B♭ | E♭ |
|--|----|---|----|----|
| I | do | mi | sol | do |

**E♭ Major Dominant Chord**

| | B♭ | D | F | B♭ |
|--|----|---|---|----|
| V | sol | ti | re | sol |

**E♭ Major Subdominant Chord**

| | A♭ | C | E♭ | A♭ |
|--|----|---|----|----|
| IV | fa | la | do | fa |

# Practice

◆ Pitch and Rhythm • E♭ Major Tonic, Dominant and Subdominant Chords

Using the E♭ major patterns below as a guide, sight-sing the following exercises separately or in any combination.

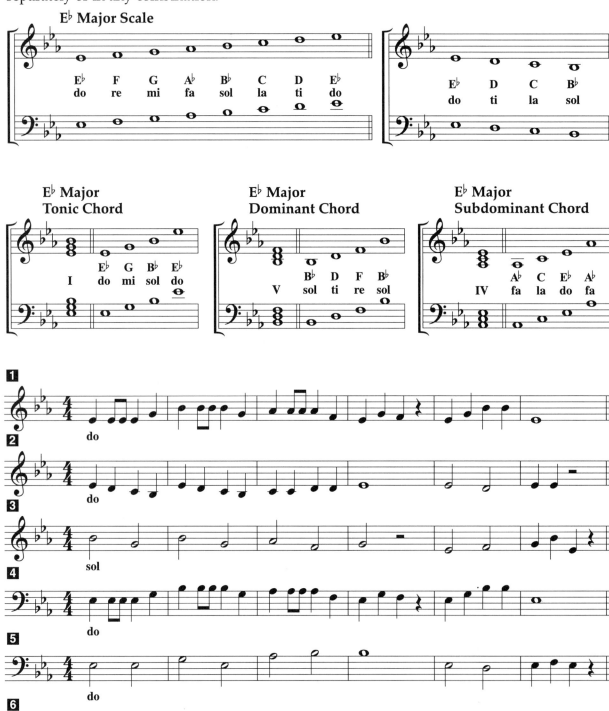

# Sing Hosanna

Words and Music by
EMILY CROCKER

# Evaluation

Demonstrate what you have learned in Chapter Ten by completing the following:

◆ Answer the following questions:
   1. The G minor scale is the relative minor of what major scale?
   2. Which flats are in the key signature of G minor?
   3. Name the notes of the G minor tonic, dominant and subdominant chords.

**G Minor
Tonic Chord**

i

**G Minor
Dominant Chord**

v

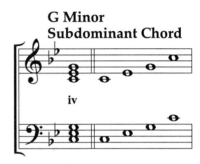

**G Minor
Subdominant Chord**

iv

## ◆ Simple or Compound Meter?
   1. In what kind of meter would triplets normally be used?
   2. In what kind of meter would duplets normally be used?

## ◆ Be A Composer
   1. Each of these rhythms equals one beat in $\frac{3}{4}$ meter. On a sheet of paper, create your own rhythm composition in $\frac{3}{4}$ meter.

   2. Each of these rhythms equals one beat in $\frac{6}{8}$ meter. On a sheet of paper, create your own rhythm composition in $\frac{6}{8}$ meter.

Add percussion instruments to your rhythm compositions. Or, create melodies by adding pitches, and transfer your compositions to a staff.

# CHAPTER 11

# Pitch

## ◆ The C Minor Scale

The minor scale is a specific arrangement of whole steps and half steps:

$$W + H + W + W + H + W + W$$

The C minor scale is a minor scale that starts and ends on C. To build this scale, begin on C and use the pattern of whole steps and half steps shown above. Notice the need for a B♭, E♭ and A♭. Play the C minor scale on the piano.

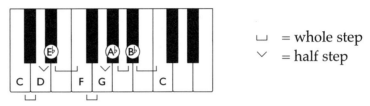

⊔ = whole step
∨ = half step

Sing the C minor scale using solfège syllables. Where do the whole steps occur? Where do the half steps occur?

The C minor scale is called the relative minor of the E♭ major scale, since both scales have the same half steps (D and E♭, *ti* and *do;* G and A♭, *mi* and *fa.*)

## ◆ Key Signature

In the key of C minor, there will always be a B♭, E♭ and A♭. The key signature for C minor looks like this:

## ◆ The C Minor Tonic, Dominant and Subdominant Chords

The **tonic chord** is *a chord built on the home tone, or keynote, of a scale.* The **dominant chord** is *a chord built on the fifth note of a scale.* The **subdominant chord** is *a chord built on the fourth note of a scale.*

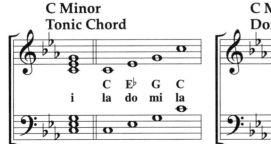

# Practice

◆ Pitch and Rhythm • C Minor Tonic, Dominant and Subdominant Chords

Using the C minor patterns below as a guide, sight-sing the following exercises separately or in any combination.

# Practice

◆ Pitch and Rhythm • C Minor Tonic, Dominant and Subdominant Chords

Using the C minor patterns below as a guide, sight-sing the following exercises separately or in any combination.

# Seasons

Words and Music by
AUDREY SNYDER

# Pitch

## ◆ The A Major Scale

The major scale is a specific arrangement of whole steps and half steps:

W + W + H + W + W + W + H

The A major scale is a major scale that starts and ends on A. To build this scale, begin on A and use the pattern of whole steps and half steps shown above. Notice the need for an F♯, C♯ and G♯. Play the A major scale on the piano.

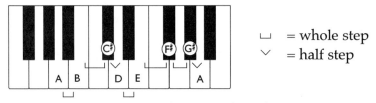

⊔ = whole step
∨ = half step

Sing the A major scale using solfège syllables. Where do the whole steps occur? Where do the half steps occur?

| A | B | C♯ | D | E | F♯ | G♯ | A | A | B | C♯ | D |
|---|---|----|---|---|----|----|---|---|---|----|---|
| do | re | mi | fa | sol | la | ti | do | do | re | mi | fa |

## ◆ Key Signature

In the key of A major, there will always be an F♯, C♯ and G♯. The key signature for A major looks like this:

## ◆ The A Major Tonic, Dominant and Subdominant Chords

The **tonic chord** is *a chord built on the home tone, or keynote, of a scale*. The **dominant chord** is *a chord built on the fifth note of a scale*. The **subdominant chord** is *a chord built on the fourth note of a scale*.

**A Major Tonic Chord**

| I | A | C♯ | E | A |
|---|---|----|---|---|
| | do | mi | sol | do |

**A Major Dominant Chord**

| V | E | G♯ | B | E |
|---|---|----|---|---|
| | sol | ti | re | sol |

**A Major Subdominant Chord**

| IV | D | F♯ | A | D |
|----|---|----|---|---|
| | fa | la | do | fa |

# Practice

◆ Pitch and Rhythm • A Major Tonic, Dominant and Subdominant Chords

Using the A major patterns below as a guide, sight-sing the following exercises separately or in any combination.

# Rhythm

◆ Time Signature • $\frac{3}{8}$ Meter

$\frac{3}{8}$ **meter** is *a time signature in which there are three beats per meaure and the eighth note receives the beat.*

$\boldsymbol{3}$  = three beats per measure

$\boldsymbol{8}$  = the eighth note receives the beat

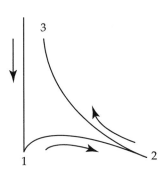

$\frac{3}{8}$ meter can be conducted in three, as shown to the right. It can also be conducted in one, if the tempo is fast.

◆ Practice

Chant the rhythms in the following exercises as you conduct.

# Practice

◆ Pitch and Rhythm • A Major in $\frac{3}{8}$ Meter

Using the A major patterns below as a guide, sight-sing the following exercises separately or in any combination.

Sing each line separately or in any combination.

# Pitch

## ◆ Altered Pitches

Sometimes, altered pitches are used in music. An **accidental** (another name for an altered pitch) is *any sharp, flat or natural that is not included in the key signature of a piece of music.* Any pitch in a scale can be altered.

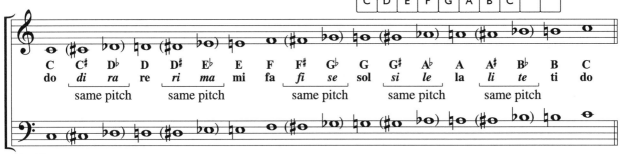

## ◆ Practice

Sight-sing the following exercises in the key of C major that use altered pitches.

### Di and Ra

Sharped *do* becomes *di*. Flatted *re* becomes *ra*.
Notice that *di* and *ra* are the same pitch.

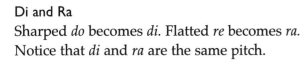

### Ri and Ma

Sharped *re* becomes *ri*. Flatted *mi* becomes *ma*.
Notice that *ri* and *ma* are the same pitch.

*The natural cancels the previous sharp.          †An altered pitch or accidental continues through the measure unless cancelled.

**Fi and Se**

Sharped *fa* becomes *fi*. Flatted *sol* becomes *se*.
Notice that *fi* and *se* are the same pitch.

**3**

**Li and Te**

Sharped *la* becomes *li*. Flatted *ti* becomes *te*.
Notice that *li* and *te* are the same pitch.

**4**

When a note which is sharped in the key signature is lowered by a half step, this note appears with a natural (♮) in the measure of music where it occurs. For example, in the key of A major, *te* appears as a note with a natural (♮), since *ti* is already a sharped note in the key signature.

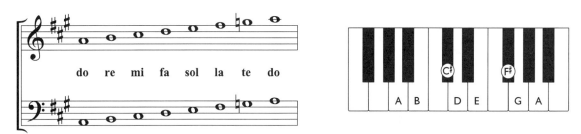

### ◆ Practice

Sight-sing the following exercise in the key of A major that uses altered pitches.

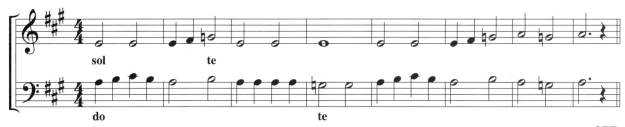

# Play, Fiddler

Words and Music by
AUDREY SNYDER

# Rhythm

## ◆ Time Signature • $\frac{6}{8}$ and $\frac{9}{8}$ Meter

**Simple meter** is *any meter in which the quarter note receives the beat and the division of the beat is based on two eighth notes.* **Compound meter** is *any meter in which the dotted quarter note receives the beat and the division of the beat is based on three eighth notes.* $\frac{6}{8}$ and $\frac{9}{8}$ meters are examples of compound meter.

**6** = two groups of three eighth notes per measure
**8** = the dotted quarter note receives the beat

$\frac{6}{8}$ meter is usually conducted in two, unless the tempo is very slow.

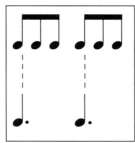 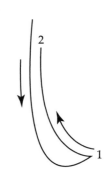

**9** = three groups of three eighth notes per measure
**8** = the dotted quarter note receives the beat

$\frac{9}{8}$ meter is usually conducted in three.

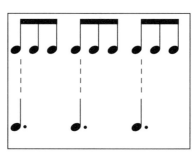 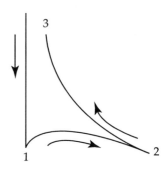

## ◆ Practice

Chant the rhythms in the following exercises as you conduct.

# Rhythm

### ◆ Time Signature • $\frac{12}{8}$ Meter

$\frac{12}{8}$ meter is another example of compound meter and is usually conducted in four.

**12** = four groups of three eighth notes per measure

**8** = the dotted quarter note receives the beat

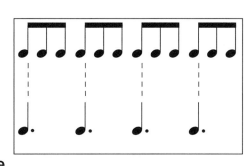
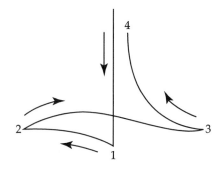

### ◆ Practice

Chant the rhythms in the following exercises as you conduct.

**1**

**2**

**3**

**4**

### ◆ Crazy Compounds

*Challenge! Keep the beat steady.*

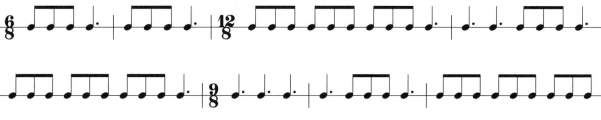

# Practice

◆ Pitch and Rhythm • A Major in $\frac{9}{8}$ and $\frac{12}{8}$ Meter

Using the A major patterns below as a guide, sight-sing the following sets of exercises in compound meter. Conduct the $\frac{9}{8}$ patterns in three and the $\frac{12}{8}$ patterns in four.

# Only A Song

Words and Music by
EMILY CROCKER

# Pitch

## ◆ Diatonic and Chromatic Scales

An **accidental** is *another name for an altered pitch.* Accidentals can be sharps, flats or naturals. An accidental is any pitch which does not occur naturally in a key. For example, G♯ would be an accidental in the key in C major.

A sharp raises
the pitch one
half step.

A flat lowers
the pitch one
half step.

A natural cancels
a previous
sharp or flat.

## ◆ Diatonic Scale

The **diatonic scale** is *a scale that uses no altered pitches or accidentals.* The major scale is an example of a diatonic scale.

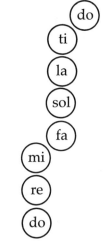

## ◆ Chromatic Scale

The **chromatic scale** is *a scale that consists of all half steps and uses all twelve pitches in an octave.*

**Chromatic Scale (ascending)**

**Chromatic Scale (descending)**

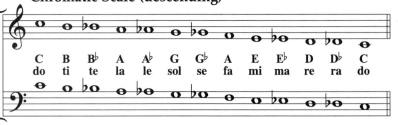

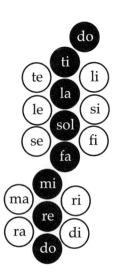

# Practice

### ◆ Pitch and Rhythm • The Chromatic Scale

Using the scales below as a guide, sight-sing the following exercises that use pitches found in the chromatic scale.

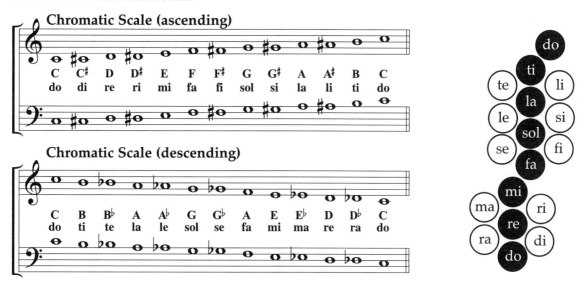

Write the chromatic scales starting on A and E on a sheet of staff paper. Then sing the following exercises.

# Pitch

## ◆ Modes and Modal Scales

Before major and minor keys and scales were developed, there was an earlier system of pitch organization called modes. Like major and minor scales, each modal scale is made up of a specific arrangement of whole steps and half steps, with the half steps occurring between *mi* and *fa*, and *ti* and *do*. Here are some examples of modal scales starting and ending on C.

Like the major scale, the **Ionian scale** is *a scale that starts and ends on* do.

∨ = half step

The **Dorian scale** is *a scale that starts and ends on* re.

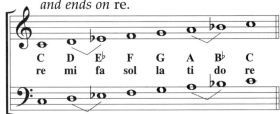

The **Phrygian scale** is *a scale that starts and ends on* mi.

The **Lydian scale** is *a scale that starts and ends on* fa.

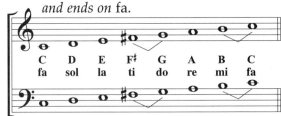

The **Mixolydian scale** is *a scale that starts and ends on* sol.

Like the minor scale, the **Aeolian scale** is *a scale that starts and ends on* la.

## ◆ Practice

Sight-sing the following melody that uses pitches found in the C Dorian scale.

# Practice

### ◆ Pitch and Rhythm • D Dorian Scale

The D Dorian scale starts and ends on D, or *re,* with half steps between E and F (*mi* and *fa*) and B and C (*ti* and *do*). Sing the D Dorian scale and then sight-sing the following exercises.

**D Dorian Scale**

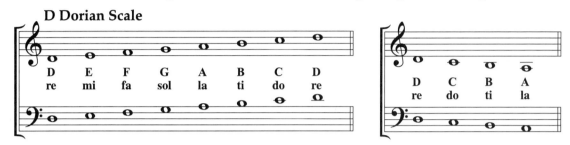

# Welcome, Welcome

Words and Music by
EMILY CROCKER

this, the fes - tive day    of days.   This, the fes - tive day    of    days.

this, the fes - tive day    of days.   This, the fes - tive day    of    days.

this, the fes - tive day    of days.   This, the fes - tive day    of    days.

On    this    fes - tive    day       of       days!

On    this    fes - tive    day       of       days!

On    this    fes - tive    day       of       days!

# Evaluation

Demonstrate what you have learned in Chapter Eleven by completing the following:

◆ **Simple Meter**
Copy the following exercises on the board or on a sheet of paper. Choose from the given rhythms and complete each measure. Clap, tap or chant while conducting the completed exercises.

◆ **Compound Meter**
Repeat the same process as above with these rhythms and the following exercises.

◆ **Chromatic Pitches**
Sight-sing the following exercise. Carefully tune the half steps.

# Evaluation

◆ Choose the best answer for the questions below:

    natural        sharp        accidental        altered pitch        flat

1. What symbol raises a pitch by a half step?
2. What symbol lowers a pitch by a half step?
3. What symbol cancels a previous sharp or flat or a sharp or flat in a key signature?
4. What two words are different names for "sharp," "flat" or "natural"?

◆ Name the notes and sing the following modal scales.

**D Dorian Scale**

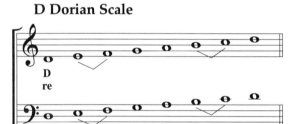

**D Mixolydian Scale**

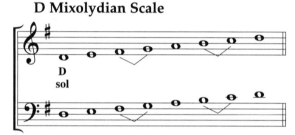

◆ Sight-sing the following melody.

# CHAPTER 12

# Pitch

### ◆ The Circle of Fifths

In music, the relationship between each key is based on a perfect fifth. A **perfect fifth** is *an interval of two pitches that are five notes apart on the staff.* An easy way to visualize this relationship is on the keyboard.

Study the keyboard below. Notice that if you start on C and move to the left by the distance of a fifth, you will find the keys that contain flats. Notice that the number of flats in each key signature increases by one each time you move one perfect fifth to the left.

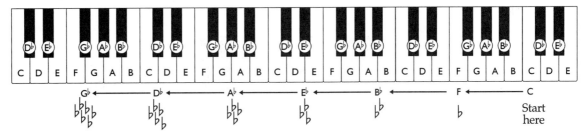

However, if you start on C and move to the right by the distance of a fifth, you will find the keys that contain sharps. Notice that the number of sharps in each key signature increases by one each time you move one perfect fifth to the right.

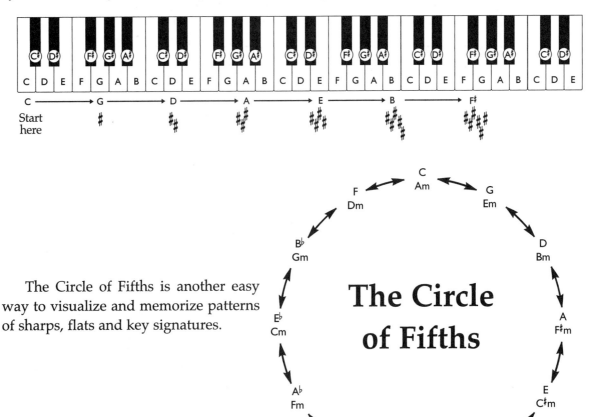

The Circle of Fifths is another easy way to visualize and memorize patterns of sharps, flats and key signatures.

# Pitch

## ◆ The A♭ Major Scale

The major scale is a specific arrangement of whole steps and half steps:

$$W + W + H + W + W + W + H$$

The A♭ major scale is a major scale that starts and ends on A♭. To build this scale, begin on A♭ and use the pattern of whole steps and half steps shown above. Notice the need for a B♭, E♭, A♭ and D♭. Play the A♭ major scale on the piano and sing this scale using solfège syllables.

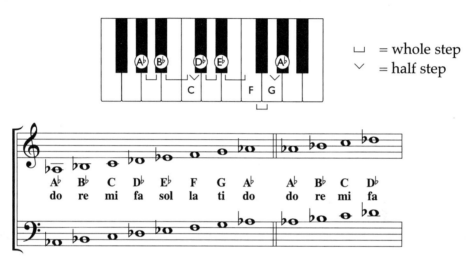

| ␄ | = whole step |
| ⌄ | = half step |

## ◆ Key Signature

In the key of A♭ major, there will always be a B♭, E♭, A♭ and D♭. The key signature for A♭ major looks like this:

## ◆ The A♭ Major Tonic, Dominant and Subdominant Chords

The **tonic chord** is *a chord built on the home tone, or keynote, of a scale.* The **dominant chord** is *a chord built on the fifth note of a scale.* The **subdominant chord** is *a chord built on the fourth note of a scale.*

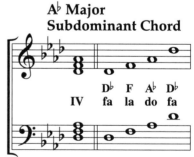

# Practice

◆ Pitch and Rhythm • Key of A♭ Major

Using the A♭ major patterns on the previous page as a guide, sight-sing the following exercises separately or in any combination.

# Pitch

## ◆ The F Minor Scale

The minor scale is a specific arrangement of whole steps and half steps:

$$W + H + W + W + H + W + W$$

The F minor scale is a minor scale that starts and ends on F. To build this scale, begin on F and use the pattern of whole steps and half steps shown above. Notice the need for a B♭, E♭, A♭ and D♭. Play the F minor scale on the piano and sing this scale using solfège syllables.

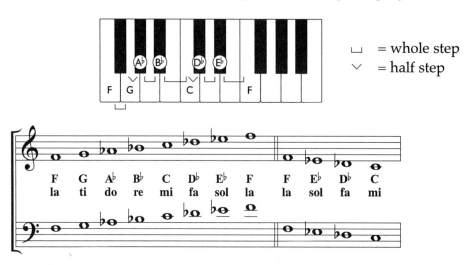

The F minor scale is called the relative minor of the A♭ major scale, since both scales have the same half steps (G and A♭, *ti* and *do*; C and D♭, *mi* and *fa*).

## ◆ Key Signature

In the key of F minor, there will always be a B♭, E♭, A♭ and D♭. The key signature for F minor looks like this:

## ◆ The F Minor Tonic, Dominant and Subdominant Chords

The **tonic chord** is *a chord built on the home tone, or keynote, of a scale.* The **dominant chord** is *a chord built on the fifth note of a scale.* The **subdominant chord** is *a chord built on the fourth note of a scale.*

**F Minor Tonic Chord**

F A♭ C F
i  la do mi la

**F Minor Dominant Chord**

C E♭ G C
v  mi sol ti mi

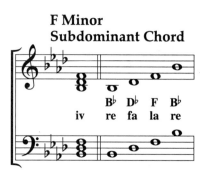

**F Minor Subdominant Chord**

B♭ D♭ F B♭
iv  re fa la re

# Practice

◆ Pitch and Rhythm • Key of F Minor
Using the F minor patterns on the previous page as a guide, sight-sing the following exercises separately or in any combination.

# Pitch

## ◆ The D♭ Major Scale

The major scale is a specific arrangement of whole steps and half steps:

$$W + W + H + W + W + W + H$$

The D♭ major scale is a major scale that starts and ends on D♭. To build this scale, begin on D♭ and use the pattern of whole steps and half steps shown above. Notice the need for a B♭, E♭, A♭, D♭ and G♭. Play the D♭ major scale on the piano and sing this scale using solfège syllables.

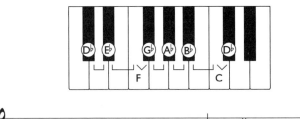

⌣ = whole step
∨ = half step

## ◆ Key Signature

In the key of D♭ major, there will always be a B♭, E♭, A♭, D♭ and G♭. The key signature for D♭ major looks like this:

## ◆ The D♭ Major Tonic, Dominant and Subdominant Chords

The **tonic chord** is *a chord built on the home tone, or keynote, of a scale.* The **dominant chord** is *a chord built on the fifth note of a scale.* The **subdominant chord** is *a chord built on the fourth note of a scale.*

**D♭ Major Tonic Chord**

I   D♭ F A♭ D♭
    do mi sol do

**D♭ Major Dominant Chord**

V   A♭ C E♭ A♭
    sol ti re sol

**D♭ Major Subdominant Chord**

IV   G♭ B♭ D♭ G♭
     fa la do fa

# Practice

### ◆ Pitch and Rhythm • Key of D♭ Major

Using the D♭ major patterns on the previous page as a guide, sight-sing the following exercises separately or in any combination.

# Pitch

## ◆ The B♭ Minor Scale

The minor scale is a specific arrangement of whole steps and half steps:

$$W + H + W + W + H + W + W$$

The B♭ minor scale is a minor scale that starts and ends on B♭. To build this scale, begin on B♭ and use the pattern of whole steps and half steps shown above. Notice the need for a B♭, E♭, A♭, D♭ and G♭. Play the B♭ minor scale on the piano and sing this scale using solfège syllables.

⌐⌐ = whole step
∨ = half step

The B♭ minor scale is called the relative minor of the D♭ major scale, since both scales have the same half steps (C and D♭, *ti* and *do*; F and G♭, *mi* and *fa*).

## ◆ Key Signature

In the key of B♭ minor, there will always be a B♭, E♭, A♭, D♭ and G♭. The key signature for B♭ minor looks like this:

## ◆ The B♭ Minor Tonic, Dominant and Subdominant Chords

The **tonic chord** is *a chord built on the home tone, or keynote, of a scale.* The **dominant chord** is *a chord built on the fifth note of a scale.* The **subdominant chord** is *a chord built on the fourth note of a scale.*

# Practice

◆ Pitch and Rhythm • Key of B♭ Minor

Using the B♭ minor patterns on the previous page as a guide, sight-sing the following exercises separately or in any combination.

# Pitch

## ◆ The G♭ Major Scale

The major scale is a specific arrangement of whole steps and half steps:

$$W + W + H + W + W + W + H$$

The G♭ major scale is a major scale that starts and ends on G♭. To build this scale, begin on G♭ and use the pattern of whole steps and half steps shown above. Notice the need for a B♭, E♭, A♭, D♭, G♭ and C♭. Play the G♭ major scale on the piano and sing this scale using solfège syllables.

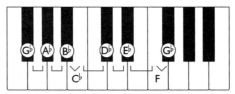

= whole step
= half step

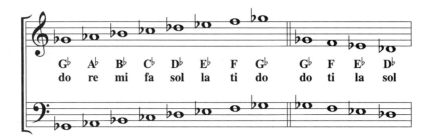

## ◆ Key Signature

In the key of G♭ major, there will always be a B♭, E♭, A♭, D♭, G♭ and C♭. The key signature for G♭ major looks like this:

## ◆ The G♭ Major Tonic, Dominant and Subdominant Chords

The **tonic chord** is *a chord built on the home tone, or keynote, of a scale*. The **dominant chord** is *a chord built on the fifth note of a scale*. The **subdominant chord** is *a chord built on the fourth note of a scale*.

G♭ Major
Tonic Chord

G♭ Major
Dominant Chord

G♭ Major
Subdominant Chord

# Practice

### ◆ Pitch and Rhythm • Key of G♭ Major

Using the G♭ major patterns on the previous page as a guide, sight-sing the following exercises separately or in any combination.

# Pitch

## ◆ The E♭ Minor Scale

The minor scale is a specific arrangement of whole steps and half steps:

W + H + W + W + H + W + W

The E♭ minor scale is a minor scale that starts and ends on E♭. To build this scale, begin on E♭ and use the pattern of whole steps and half steps shown above. Notice the need for a B♭, E♭, A♭, D♭, G♭ and C♭. Play the E♭ minor scale on the piano and sing this scale using solfège syllables.

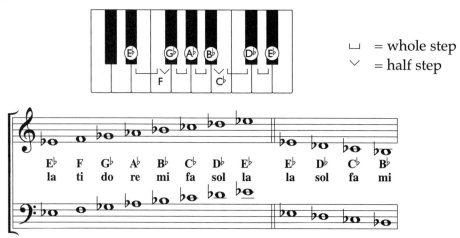

⌐ = whole step
∨ = half step

The E♭ minor scale is called the relative minor of the G♭ major scale, since both scales have the same half steps (F and G♭, *ti* and *do*; B♭ and C♭, *mi* and *fa*).

## ◆ Key Signature

In the key of E♭ minor, there will always be a B♭, E♭, A♭, D♭, G♭ and C♭. The key signature for E♭ minor looks like this:

## ◆ The E♭ Minor Tonic, Dominant and Subdominant Chords

The **tonic chord** is *a chord built on the home tone, or keynote, of a scale*. The **dominant chord** is *a chord built on the fifth note of a scale*. The **subdominant chord** is *a chord built on the fourth note of a scale*.

E♭ Minor
Tonic Chord

E♭ G♭ B♭ E♭
i  la do mi la

E♭ Minor
Dominant Chord

B♭ D♭ F B♭
v  mi sol ti mi

E♭ Minor
Subdominant Chord

A♭ C♭ E♭ A♭
iv  re fa la re

# Practice

◆ Pitch and Rhythm • Key of E♭ Minor

Using the E♭ minor patterns on the previous page as a guide, sight-sing the following exercises separately or in any combination.

# Pitch

## ◆ The E Major Scale

The major scale is a specific arrangement of whole steps and half steps:

$$W + W + H + W + W + W + H$$

The E major scale is a major scale that starts and ends on E.  To build this scale, begin on E and use the pattern of whole steps and half steps shown above. Notice the need for an F♯, C♯, G♯ and D♯. Play the E major scale on the piano  and sing this scale using solfège syllables.

⎵ = whole step
∨ = half step

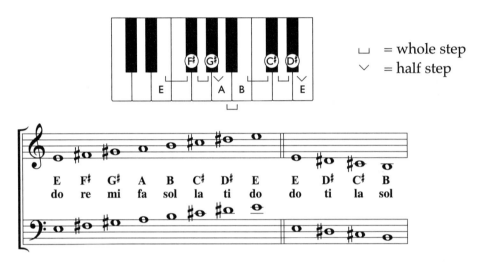

## ◆ Key Signature

In the key of E major, there will always be an F♯, C♯, G♯ and  D♯. The key signature for E major looks like this:

## ◆ The E Major Tonic, Dominant and Subdominant Chords

The **tonic chord** is *a chord built on the home tone, or keynote, of a scale.* The **dominant chord** is *a chord built on the fifth note of a scale.* The **subdominant chord** is *a chord built on the fourth note of a scale.*

**E Major Tonic Chord**

| E | G♯ | B | E |
|---|---|---|---|
| do | mi | sol | do |

I

**E Major Dominant Chord**

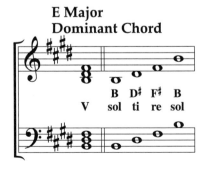

| B | D♯ | F♯ | B |
|---|---|---|---|
| sol | ti | re | sol |

V

**E Major Subdominant Chord**

| A | C♯ | E | A |
|---|---|---|---|
| fa | la | do | fa |

IV

# Practice

◆ Pitch and Rhythm • Key of E Major

Using the E major patterns on the previous page as a guide, sight-sing the following exercises separately or in any combination.

# Pitch

## ◆ The C♯ Minor Scale

The minor scale is a specific arrangement of whole steps and half steps:

$$W + H + W + W + H + W + W$$

The C♯ minor scale is a minor scale that starts and ends on C♯. To build this scale, begin on C♯ and use the pattern of whole steps and half steps shown above. Notice the need for an F♯, C♯, G♯ and D♯. Play the C♯ minor scale on the piano and sing this scale using solfège syllables.

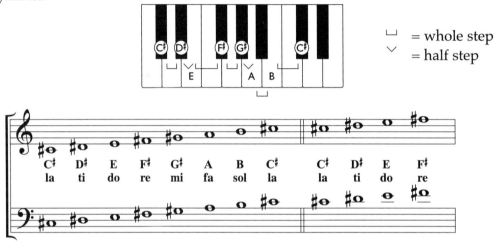

The C♯ minor scale is called the relative minor of the E major scale, since both scales have the same half steps (D♯ and E, *ti* and *do*; G♯ and A, *mi* and *fa*).

## ◆ Key Signature

In the key of C♯ minor, there will always be an F♯, C♯, G♯ and D♯. The key signature for C♯ minor looks like this:

## ◆ The C♯ Minor Tonic, Dominant and Subdominant Chords

The **tonic chord** is *a chord built on the home tone, or keynote, of a scale.* The **dominant chord** is *a chord built on the fifth note of a scale.* The **subdominant chord** is *a chord built on the fourth note of a scale.*

# Practice

◆ Pitch and Rhythm • Key of C♯ Minor

Using the C♯ minor patterns on the previous page as a guide, sight-sing the following exercises separately or in any combination.

# Pitch

## ◆ The B Major Scale

The major scale is a specific arrangement of whole steps and half steps:

W + W + H + W + W + W + H

The B major scale is a major scale that starts and ends on B. To build this scale, begin on B and use the pattern of whole steps and half steps shown above. Notice the need for an F♯, C♯, G♯, D♯ and A♯. Play the B major scale on the piano and sing this scale using solfège syllables.

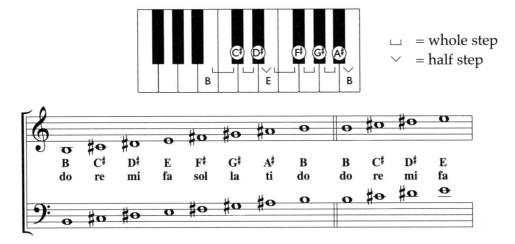

## ◆ Key Signature

In the key of B major, there will always be an F♯, C♯, G♯, D♯ and A♯. The key signature for B major looks like this:

## ◆ The B Major Tonic, Dominant and Subdominant Chords

The **tonic chord** is *a chord built on the home tone or keynote of a scale.* The **dominant chord** is *a chord built on the fifth note of a scale.* The **subdominant chord** is *a chord built on the fourth note of a scale.*

B Major
Tonic Chord

B Major
Dominant Chord

B Major
Subdominant Chord

# Practice

◆ Pitch and Rhythm • Key of B Major

Using the B major patterns on the previous page as a guide, sight-sing the following exercises separately or in any combination.

# Pitch

## ◆ The G♯ Minor Scale

The minor scale is a specific arrangement of whole steps and half steps:

$$W + H + W + W + H + W + W$$

The G♯ minor scale is a minor scale that starts and ends on G♯. To build this scale, begin on G♯ and use the pattern of whole steps and half steps shown above. Notice the need for an F♯, C♯, G♯, D♯ and A♯. Play the G♯ minor scale on the piano and sing this scale using solfège syllables.

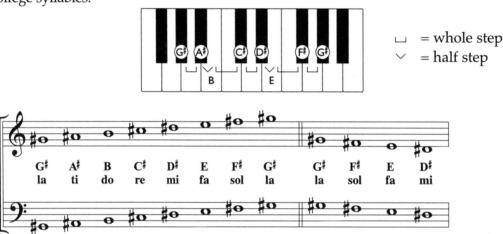

The G♯ minor scale is called the relative minor of the B major scale, since both scales have the same half steps (A♯ and B, *ti* and *do*; D♯ and E, *mi* and *fa*).

## ◆ Key Signature

In the key of G♯ minor, there will always be an F♯, C♯, G♯, D♯ and A♯. The key signature for G♯ minor looks like this:

## ◆ The G♯ Minor Tonic, Dominant and Subdominant Chords

The **tonic chord** is *a chord built on the home tone, or keynote, of a scale*. The **dominant chord** is *a chord built on the fifth note of a scale*. The **subdominant chord** is *a chord built on the fourth note of a scale*.

# Practice

◆ Pitch and Rhythm • Key of G♯ Minor

Using the G♯ minor patterns on the previous page as a guide, sight-sing the following exercises separately or in any combination.

# Pitch

## ◆ The F♯ Major Scale

The major scale is a specific arrangement of whole steps and half steps:

$$W + W + H + W + W + W + H$$

The F♯ major scale is a major scale that starts and ends on F♯. To build this scale, begin on F♯ and use the pattern of whole steps and half steps shown above. Notice the need for an F♯, C♯, G♯, D♯, A♯ and E♯. Play the F♯ major scale on the piano and sing this scale using solfège syllables.

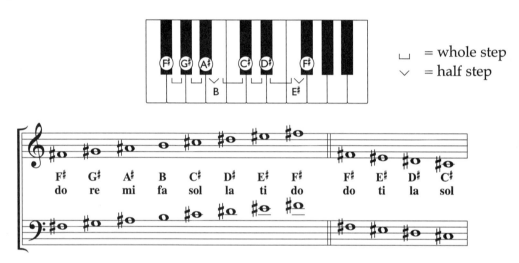

= whole step
= half step

## ◆ Key Signature

In the key of F♯ major, there will always be an F♯, C♯, G♯, D♯, A♯ and E♯. The key signature for F♯ major looks like this:

## ◆ The F♯ Major Tonic, Dominant and Subdominant Chords

The **tonic chord** is *a chord built on the home tone, or keynote, of a scale.* The **dominant chord** is *a chord built on the fifth note of a scale.* The **subdominant chord** is *a chord built on the fourth note of a scale.*

**F♯ Major Tonic Chord**

F♯ A♯ C♯ F♯
I   do mi sol do

**F♯ Major Dominant Chord**

C♯ E♯ G♯ C♯
V   sol ti re sol

**F♯ Major Subdominant Chord**

B D♯ F♯ B
IV fa la do fa

# Practice

◆ Pitch and Rhythm • Key of F♯ Major

Using the F♯ major patterns on the previous page as a guide, sight-sing the following exercises separately or in any combination.

# Pitch

### ◆ The D♯ Minor Scale

The minor scale is a specific arrangement of whole steps and half steps:

W + H + W + W + H + W + W

The D♯ minor scale is a minor scale that starts and ends on D♯. To build this scale, begin on D♯ and use the pattern of whole steps and half steps shown above. Notice the need for an F♯, C♯, G♯, D♯, A♯ and E♯. Play the D♯ minor scale on the piano and sing this scale using solfège syllables.

⌣ = whole step
⌄ = half step

The D♯ minor scale is called the relative minor of the F♯ major scale, since both scales have the same half steps (E♯ and F♯, *ti* and *do*; A♯ and B, *mi* and *fa*).

### ◆ Key Signature

In the key of D♯ minor, there will always be an F♯, C♯, G♯, D♯, A♯ and E♯. The key signature for D♯ minor looks like this:

### ◆ The D♯ Minor Tonic, Dominant and Subdominant Chords

The **tonic chord** is *a chord built on the home tone, or keynote, of a scale.* The **dominant chord** is *a chord built on the fifth note of a scale.* The **subdominant chord** is *a chord built on the fourth note of a scale.*

**D♯ Minor Tonic Chord**

**D♯ Minor Dominant Chord**

**D♯ Minor Subdominant Chord**

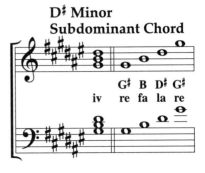

# Practice

◆ Pitch and Rhythm • Key of D♯ Minor

Using the D♯ minor patterns on the previous page as a guide, sight-sing the following exercises separately or in any combination.

# Evaluation

Demonstrate what you have learned in Chapter Twelve by completing the following:

◆ Answer the following questions:
   1. The key signature for A major has how many sharps?
   2. The key signature for F major has how many flats?
   3. The key signature for E major has how many sharps?

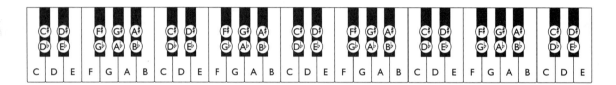

◆ ## Tire Troubles
Sight-sing the following melodies. What key is each in?

Did You See The Sharp Rock In The Road?

Got A Flat Tire!

I Always Trust My Spare Tire That Will Never Be Flat

# Appendix

# To The Teacher

*EXPERIENCING CHORAL MUSIC–Intermediate Sight-Singing* is designed to provide a sequential program to be used in the choral classroom for the study of music theory and music reading skills. For students to gain the most from this material, plan 10–15 minutes of daily study, including the introduction of new material, as well as the practice and review of previous material.

## ◆ Features of the Program
- The sequence is pedagogically sound and practical.
- The terminology is accurate and literal.
- Music theory is presented in a format that is compatible with the material in the *EXPERIENCING CHORAL MUSIC* repertoire books. Cross-references are provided in each repertoire book to the coordinating concepts in this book.
- It is designed to be successful within a variety of choral organizations: treble, tenor/bass or mixed.

# How To Use This Book

*EXPERIENCING CHORAL MUSIC–Intermediate Sight-Singing* is organized into 12 chapters that include material for developing skills in music theory, sight-singing melodic exercises, and sight-reading rhythmic exercises. Songs to sight-sing that cover the concepts introduced in each chapter are also included. Various musical terms and symbols are introduced. Finally, each chapter concludes with a comprehensive evaluation.

## ◆ Sight-Singing
The sight-singing exercises and songs are designed to allow students to practice the concepts presented in each chapter. Included in this material are:
- Various musical terms and symbols.
- The use of solfège syllables to identify and sing correct pitches.
- Echo-singing and group practice exercises.
- Combinable exercises that provide practice in unison sight-singing and part-singing.

## ◆ Methods of Sight-Singing
There are many good methods to use in developing sight-singing skills. For the melodic exercises, consider using numbers or solfège syllables (movable or fixed *do*). For rhythm reading, consider the Eastman, Traditional or Kodály methods. It is important to be consistent and use the same method daily. More information about each method is included in this Appendix.

# National Standards Middle School Grades 5–8

The National Standards for Music Education were developed by the Music Educators National Conference. Reprinted by permission.

## Music

The period represented by grades 5–8 is especially critical in students' musical development. The music they perform or study often becomes an integral part of their personal musical repertoire. Composing and improvising provide students with unique insight into the form and structure of music and at the same time help them develop their creativity. Broad experience with a variety of music is necessary if students are to make informed musical judgments. Similarly, this breadth of background enables them to begin to understand the connections and relationships between music and other disciplines. By understanding the cultural and historical forces that shape social attitudes and behaviors, students are better prepared to live and work in communities that are increasingly multi-cultural. The role that music will play in students' lives depends in large measure on the level of skills they achieve in creating, performing and listening to music.

*Every course in music, including performance courses, should provide instruction in creating, performing, listening to and analyzing music, in addition to focusing on its specific subject matter.*

1.  **Content Standard:** Singing, alone and with others, a varied repertoire of music
    **Achievement Standard:**
    Students
    a.  sing accurately and with good breath control throughout their singing ranges, alone and in small and large ensembles
    b.  sing with *expression and *technical accuracy a repertoire of vocal literature with a *level of difficulty of 2, on a scale of 1 to 6, including some songs performed from memory
    c.  sing music representing diverse *genres and cultures, with expression appropriate for the work being performed
    d.  sing music written in two and three parts
    Students who participate in a choral ensemble
    e.  sing with expression and technical accuracy a varied repertoire of vocal literature with a level of difficulty of 3, on a scale of 1 to 6, including some songs performed from memory

2.  **Content Standard:** Performing on instruments, alone and with others, a varied repertoire of music
    **Achievement Standard:**
    Students
    a.  perform on at least one instrument[1] accurately and independently, alone and in small and large ensembles, with good posture, good playing position and good breath, bow or stick control
    b.  perform with expression and technical accuracy on at least one string, wind, percussion or *classroom instrument a repertoire of instrumental literature

with a level of difficulty of 2, on a scale of 1 to 6

    c. perform music representing diverse genres and cultures, with expression appropriate for the work being performed

    d. play by ear simple melodies on a melodic instrument and simple accompaniments on a harmonic instrument

Students who participate in an instrumental ensemble or class

    e. perform with expression and technical accuracy a varied repertoire of instrumental literature with a level of difficulty of 3, on a scale of 1 to 6, including some solos performed from memory

3. **Content Standard:** Improvising melodies, variations and accompaniments
   **Achievement Standard:**
   Students

    a. improvise simple harmonic accompaniments

    b. improvise melodic embellishments and simple rhythmic and melodic variations on given pentatonic melodies and melodies in major keys

    c. improvise short melodies, unaccompanied and over given rhythmic accompaniments, each in a consistent *style, *meter and *tonality

4. **Content Standard:** Composing and arranging music within specified guidelines
   **Achievement Standard:**
   Students

    a. compose short pieces within specified guidelines,[2] demonstrating how the elements of music are used to achieve unity and variety, tension and release, and balance

    b. arrange simple pieces for voices or instruments other than those for which the pieces were written

    c. use a variety of traditional and nontraditional sound sources and electronic media when composing and arranging

5. **Content Standard:** Reading and notating music
   **Achievement Standard:**
   Students

    a. read whole, half, quarter, eighth, sixteenth and dotted notes and rests in 2/4, 3/4, 4/4, 6/8, 3/8 and *alla breve meter signatures

    b. read at sight simple melodies in both the treble and bass clefs

    c. identify and define standard notation symbols for pitch, rhythm, *dynamics, tempo, *articulation and expression

    d. use standard notation to record their musical ideas and the musical ideas of others

6. **Content Standard:** Listening to, analyzing and describing music
   **Achievement Standard:**
   Students

    a. describe specific music events[3] in a given aural example, using appropriate terminology

    b. analyze the uses of *elements of music in aural examples representing diverse genres and cultures

    c. demonstrate knowledge of the basic principles of meter, rhythm, tonality, intervals, chords and harmonic progressions in the analyses of music

7. **Content Standard:**  Evaluating music and music performances
   **Achievement Standard:**
   Students
   > a.  develop criteria for evaluating the quality and effectiveness of music performances and compositions and apply criteria in their personal listening and performing
   > b.  evaluate the quality and effectiveness of their own and others' performances, compositions, arrangements and improvisations by applying specific criteria appropriate for the style of the music and offer constructive suggestions for improvement

8. **Content Standard:**  Understanding relationships between music, the other arts and disciplines outside the arts
   **Achievement Standard:**
   Students
   > a.  compare in two or more arts how the characteristic materials of each art (that is, sound in music, visual stimuli in visual arts, movement in dance, human interrelationships in theatre) can be used to transform similar events, scenes, emotions or ideas into works of art
   > b.  describe ways in which the principles and subject matter of other disciplines taught in the school are interrelated with those of music[4]

9. **Content Standard:**  Understanding music in relation to history and culture
   **Achievement Standard:**
   Students
   > a.  describe distinguishing characteristics of representative music genres and styles from a variety of cultures
   > b.  classify by genre and style (and, if applicable, by historical period, composer and title) a varied body of exemplary (that is, high-quality and characteristic) musical works and explain the characteristics that cause each work to be considered exemplary
   > c.  compare, in several cultures of the world, functions music serves, roles of musicians[5] and conditions under which music is typically performed

Terms identified by an asterisk (*) are explained further in the glossary of *National Standards for Arts Education,* published by Music Educators National Conference, © 1994.

1. E.g., band or orchestra instrument, *fretted instrument, electronic instrument
2. E.g., a particular style, form, instrumentation, compositional technique
3. E.g., entry of oboe, change of meter, return of refrain
4. E.g., language arts: issues to be considered in setting texts to music; mathematics: frequency ratios of intervals; sciences: the human hearing process and hazards to hearing; social studies: historical and social events and movements chronicled in or influenced by musical works
5. E.g., lead guitarist in a rock band, composer of jingles for commercials, singer in Peking opera

# National Standards High School Grades 9–12

The National Standards for Music Education were developed by the Music Educators National Conference. Reprinted by permission.

## Music

The study of music contributes in important ways to the quality of every student's life. Every musical work is a product of its time and place, although some works transcend their original settings and continue to appeal to humans through their timeless and universal attraction. Through singing, playing instruments and composing, students can express themselves creatively, while a knowledge of notation and performance traditions enables them to learn new music independently throughout their lives. Skills in analysis, evaluation and synthesis are important because they enable students to recognize and pursue excellence in the musical experiences and to understand and enrich their environment. Because music is an integral part of human history, the ability to listen with understanding is essential if students are to gain a broad cultural and historical perspective. The adult life of every student is enriched by the skills, knowledge and habits acquired in the study of music.

*Every course in music, including performance courses, should provide instruction in creating, performing, listening to and analyzing music, in addition to focusing on its specific subject matter.*

1. **Content Standard:** Singing, alone and with others, a varied repertoire of music
   **Achievement Standard, Proficient:**
   Students
   a. sing with *expression and *technical accuracy a large and varied repertoire of vocal literature with a *level of difficulty of 4, on a scale of 1 to 6, including some songs performed from memory
   b. sing music written in four parts, with and without accompaniment
   c. demonstrate well-developed ensemble skills

2. **Content Standard:** Performing on instruments, alone and with others, a varied repertoire of music
   **Achievement Standard, Proficient:**
   Students
   a. perform with expression and technical accuracy a large and varied repertoire of instrumental literature with a level of difficulty of 4, on a scale of 1 to 6
   b. perform an appropriate part in an ensemble, demonstrating well-developed ensemble skills
   c. perform in small ensembles with one student on a part

3. **Content Standard:** Improvising melodies, variations and accompaniments
   **Achievement Standard, Proficient:**
   Students
      a. improvise stylistically appropriate harmonizing parts
      b. improvise rhythmic and melodic variations on given pentatonic melodies and melodies in major and minor keys
      c. improvise original melodies over given chord progressions, each in a consistent *style, *meter and *tonality

4. **Content Standard:** Composing and arranging music within specified guidelines
   **Achievement Standard, Proficient:**
   Students
      a. compose music in several distinct styles, demonstrating creativity in using the *elements of music for expressive effect
      b. arrange pieces for voices or instruments other than those for which the pieces were written in ways that preserve or enhance the expressive effect of the music
      c. compose and arrange music for voices and various acoustic and electronic instruments, demonstrating knowledge of the ranges and traditional usages of the sound sources

5. **Content Standard:** Reading and notating music
   **Achievement Standard, Proficient:**
   Students
      a. demonstrate the ability to read an instrumental or vocal score of up to four *staves by describing how the elements of music are used
   Students who participate in a choral or instrumental ensemble or class
      b. sight-read, accurately and expressively, music with a level of difficulty of 3, on a scale of 1 to 6

6. **Content Standard:** Listening to, analyzing and describing music
   **Achievement Standard, Proficient:**
   Students
      a. analyze aural examples of a varied repertoire of music, representing diverse *genres and cultures, by describing the uses of elements of music and expressive devices
      b. demonstrate extensive knowledge of the technical vocabulary of music
      c. identify and explain compositional devices and techniques used to provide unity and variety and tension and release in a musical work and give examples of other works that make similar uses of these devices and techniques

7. **Content Standard:** Evaluating music and music performances
   **Achievement Standard, Proficient:**
   Students
      a. evolve specific criteria for making informed, critical evaluations of the quality

and effectiveness of performances, compositions, arrangements and improvisations and apply the criteria in their personal participation in music

    b. evaluate a performance, composition, arrangement or improvisation by comparing it to similar or exemplary models

8. **Content Standard:** Understanding relationships between music, the other arts, and disciplines outside the arts
   **Achievement Standard, Proficient:**
   Students
   
       a. explain how elements, artistic processes (such as imagination or craftsmanship), and organizational principles (such as unity and variety or repetition and contrast) are used in similar and distinctive ways in the various arts and cite examples
   
       b. compare characteristics of two or more arts within a particular historical period or style and cite examples from various cultures
   
       c. explain ways in which the principles and subject matter of various disciplines outside the arts are interrelated with those of music[1]

9. **Content Standard:** Understanding music in relation to history and culture
   **Achievement Standard, Proficient:**
   Students
   
       a. classify by genre or style and by historical period or culture unfamiliar but representative aural examples of music and explain the reasoning behind their classifications
   
       b. identify sources of American music genres,[2] trace the evolution of those genres, and cite well-known musicians associated with them
   
       c. identify various roles[3] that musicians perform, cite representative individuals who have functioned in each role, and describe their activities and achievements

Terms identified by an asterisk (*) are explained further in the glossary of *National Standards for Arts Education*, published by Music Educators National Conference, © 1994.

1. E.g., language arts: compare the ability of music and literature to convey images, feeling and meanings; physics: describe the physical basis of tone production in string, wind, percussion and electronic instruments and the human voice and of the transmission and perception of sound
2. E.g., swing, Broadway musical, blues
3. E.g., entertainer, teacher, transmitter of cultural tradition

# CHAPTER OVERVIEWS • FOCUSES • EVALUATION ANSWERS

## Book Overview

Throughout this book, a concept in rhythm, pitch or terminology is presented. Exercises for drill and practice of the concept follow. These exercises may be in the form of echo singing, practice exercises or combinable lines (lines that may be sung individually or in any combination). Then, a sight-singing song is provided that places the new concepts in the context of a song. By sight-singing the song successfully, students demonstrate mastery of the new concept. The Evaluation section at the end of the chapter is a comprehensive assessment of the concepts presented in the chapter.

## Chapter One Overview

In Chapter One, the staff, treble clef and bass clef, the grand staff, barline, measure, double barline and repeat sign are introduced. The rhythmic concepts of beat, quarter note and rest, half note and rest, dotted half note and whole note and rest are presented along with time signature and 4/4 meter. In the area of pitch, the concepts of the major scale and the key of C major are covered.

### Chapter One Focus

- Read quarter, half, dotted half, and whole notes and rests in 4/4 meter. (*NS 5a*)
- Read at sight simple melodies in treble clef and bass clef. (*NS 5b*)
- Identify and define standard notation symbols for pitch and rhythm. (*NS 5c*)

### Chapter One Evaluation

Answers to Questions on page 14:
- *First Bullet: Name the Notes*
  The first five notes of the C major scale are C, D, E, F, G or *do, re, mi, fa, sol.*
- *Second Bullet: 4/4 Meter*
  In 4/4 meter, the top number means there are four beats in a measure and the bottom number means that the quarter note receives the beat.
- *Third Bullet: Name the Kind of Notes*
  The names of the notes and rests from left to right are **(a)** half note; **(b)** whole note; **(c)** quarter note; **(d)** dotted half note; **(e)** quarter rest; **(f)** whole rest; **(g)** half rest.
- *Fourth Bullet: 4/4 Meter Equivalents*
  Based on 4/4 meter:
  **(1)** two quarter notes are equal to the same amount of time as one half note; **(2)** a dotted half note equals the same amount of time as three quarter notes; **(3)** a whole note receives four beats.
- *Fifth Bullet: Sight-Singing Exercises*
  Check for accurate pitch and rhythm while maintaining a steady beat.

## Chapter Two Overview

In Chapter Two, the concept of 3/4 meter is introduced, as well as the C major and A minor scales. Practice exercises and sight-singing songs are provided in 3/4 meter for both C major and A minor.

### Chapter Two Focus

- Compose short pieces within specified guidelines. (*NS 4a*)
- Read notation in 3/4 and 4/4 meters (*NS 5a*)
- Read at sight simple melodies in treble clef and bass clef. (*NS 5b*)
- Identify and define standard notation symbols for pitch and rhythm. (*NS 5c*)
- Use standard notation to record musical ideas. (*NS 5d*)

## Chapter Two Evaluation
Answers to Questions on page 25:
- *First Bullet: Name the Notes*

  The notes in the C major scale are: C, D, E, F, G, A, B, C or *do, re, mi, fa, sol, la, ti, do*. The half steps occur between E and F (*mi* and *fa*) and between B and C (*ti* and *do*). The notes in the A minor scale are: A, B, C, D, E, F, G, A or *la, ti, do, re, mi, fa, sol, la*. The half steps occur between B and C (*ti* and *do*) and between E and F (*mi* and *fa*).
- *Second Bullet: Sight-Singing Melodies*

  Check for accurate pitch and rhythm while maintaining a steady beat.
- *Third Bullet: Be A Composer*

  Each composition will be different. Check for correct pitch and rhythm. Give students the opportunity to play their compositions on a keyboard and review/discuss lyric choices.

## Chapter Three Overview
In Chapter Three, eighth notes and rests, as well as grouped eighth notes, are presented for the first time. In the key of C major, the tonic chord is introduced. More C major study is featured in combinable lines and a sight-singing song in 4/4 meter. Similar material is presented in the key of A minor, including the tonic chord, combinable lines in 3/4 and 4/4 meters, and a sight-singing song. Tied notes are also presented.

### Chapter Three Focus
- Read notation including eighth notes and rests. *(NS 5a)*
- Read at sight simple melodies in treble clef and bass clef. *(NS 5b)*
- Identify and define standard notation symbols for pitch and rhythm. *(NS 5c)*

### Chapter Three Evaluation
Answers to Questions on page 38:
- *First Bullet: Name the Notes*

  The note names for the C major tonic chord

are: C, E, G, C or *do, mi, sol, do*. The note names for the A minor tonic chord are: A, C, E, A or *la, do, mi, la*.
- *Second Bullet: How Many Beats?*

  When the quarter note receives the beat: **(a)** one quarter note tied to another quarter note equals two beats; **(b)** one half note tied to one quarter note equals three beats; **(c)** one half note tied to one dotted half note equals five beats; **(d)** one whole note tied to one half note equals six beats.
- *Third Bullet: Sight-Singing Exercises*

  Check for accuracy of pitch and rhythm while maintaining a steady beat.

## Chapter Four Overview
In Chapter Four, the F major and D minor scales and tonic chords are introduced. Tied notes are reviewed. Dotted half and quarter notes are introduced. Pitch and rhythm combinable lines in each key are found in 3/4 and 4/4 meters. Common terms and symbols for dynamics are introduced and then applied in a speech chorus. Sight-singing songs in F major and D minor are featured.

### Chapter Four Focus
- Read notation including dotted quarter notes in 3/4 and 4/4 meters. *(NS 5a)*
- Read at sight simple melodies in treble clef and bass clef. *(NS 5b)*
- Identify and define standard notation symbols for pitch, rhythm, and dynamics. *(NS 5c)*

### Chapter Four Evaluation
Answers to Questions on page 56:
- *First Bullet: Musical Math*

  When the quarter note receives the beat: **(a)** one half note plus one quarter note equals three beats; **(b)** one quarter note plus one eighth note equals one and a half beats; **(c)** one dotted half note plus one quarter note equals four beats; **(d)** one dotted half note equals three beats; **(e)** one dotted quarter note equals one and a half beats; **(f)** one dotted quarter note plus one eighth note equals two beats.

- *Second Bullet: Rhythm Exercises*
  Check for accurate rhythm while maintaining a steady beat.
- *Third Bullet: Sight-Singing Exercise*
  Check for accurate pitch and rhythm while maintaining a steady beat.
- *Fourth Bullet: Sight-Singing Melody*
  Check for accurate pitch and rhythm while maintaining a steady beat.

## Chapter Five Overview

In Chapter Five, the concepts of sixteenth notes, 2/4 meter, and dominant chords are introduced. The rhythmic concept of sixteenth and eighth note combinations is presented and is followed by two speech choruses that contain the combinations. Combinable lines in the keys of F major and D minor are provided. The tonic and dominant chords in C major and A minor are presented. The natural, harmonic and melodic minor scales are introduced. Sight-singing songs are provided.

### Chapter Five Focus
- Compose short pieces within specified guidelines. *(NS 4a)*
- Read notation, including sixteenth notes and sixteenth and eighth note combinations. *(NS 5a)*
- Read at sight simple melodies in treble clef and bass clef. *(NS 5b)*
- Identify and define standard notation symbols for pitch, rhythm, and dynamics. *(NS 5c)*
- Use standard notation to record musical ideas. *(NS 5d)*

### Chapter Five Evaluation
Answers to Questions on page 74:
- *First Bullet: Reviewing Rhythm and Chords*
  **(1)** When the quarter note receives the beat, there are four sixteenth notes per beat; **(2)** tonic chord; **(3)** dominant chord.
- *Second Bullet: Sight-Singing Melodies*
  Check for accurate pitch and rhythm while maintaining a steady beat.

### Chapter Five Evaluation
Answers to Questions on page 75:
- *First Bullet: Name the Notes*
  **(a)** the C major tonic chord note names are: C, E, G, C or *do, mi, sol, do;* **(b)** the C major dominant chord note names are G, B, D, or *sol, ti, re;* **(c)** the A minor tonic chord note names are A, C, E, A or *la, do, mi, la;* **(d)** the A minor dominant (raised 7th) chord note names are E, G♯, B, E or *mi, si, ti, mi.*
- *Second Bullet: Sight-Singing Melody*
  Check for accurate pitch and rhythm while maintaining a steady beat.
- *Third Bullet: Be A Composer*
  Each composition will be different. Check for correct pitch and rhythm.

## Chapter Six Overview

In Chapter Six, the F major and D minor tonic and dominant chords are presented. The G major scale is introduced with the G major tonic and dominant chords. Practice exercises in 4/4, 3/4, and 2/4 meter in all keys are provided. Sight-singing songs are included.

### Chapter Six Focus
- Read notation in 4/4, 3/4 and 2/4 meters. *(NS 5a)*
- Read at sight simple melodies in treble clef and bass clef. *(NS 5b)*
- Identify standard notation symbols for pitch and rhythm. *(NS 5c)*

## Chapter Six Evaluation

Answers to Questions on page 88:

- *First Bullet:  In the Key of D Minor*
  **(1)** the tonic note is D or *la*; **(2)** the dominant note is A or *mi*.
- *Second Bullet: In the Key of G Major*
  **(1)** the tonic note is G or *do*; **(2)** the dominant note is D or *sol*.
- *Third Bullet: Musical Math*
  **(a)** four sixteenth notes equal the same amount of time as two eighth notes; **(b)** a combination of one eighth note and two sixteenth notes equals the same amount of time as one quarter note.
- *Fourth Bullet:  True or False*
  True: an eighth rest and two sixteenth notes equals the same amount of time as two sixteenth notes combined with an eighth note.
- *Fifth Bullet: Sight-Singing Melody*
  **(1)** Key of D minor; **(2)** Key of G major; **(3)** Key of G major; **(4)** Key of D minor.  Check for accurate pitch and rhythm while maintaining a steady beat.

## Chapter Seven Overview

In Chapter Seven, the rhythmic concepts of dotted eighth and sixteenth note combinations, mixed meter, and swing rhythms are presented.  A speech chorus in mixed meter is included to reinforce the concept.  The E minor (natural and melodic), D major and B minor (natural and melodic) scales are introduced, as well as the tonic and dominant chords in each key.  Practice exercises and combinable lines in 2/4, 3/4 and 4/4 meters and sight-singing songs are used throughout the chapter.

## Chapter Seven Focus

- Compose short pieces within specified guidelines. *(NS 4a)*
- Read notation, including dotted eighth and sixteenth note combinations. *(NS 5a)*
- Read at sight simple melodies in treble clef and bass clef. *(NS 5b)*
- Identify standard notation symbols for pitch and rhythm. *(NS 5c)*
- Use standard notation to record musical ideas. *(NS 5d)*

## Chapter Seven Evaluation

Answers to Questions on page 108:

- *First Bullet:  Which Rhythm?*
  Direct the class to perform exercises 1-4. Then, have students challenge each other as described on the page.
- *Second Bullet:  Write-A-Rhythm*
  Each rhythm composition will be different. Check for number of beats per measure and correct rhythms.
- *Third Bullet:  Which Meter?*
  **(Line 1)** 4/4 meter; **(Line 2)** 3/4 meter; **(Line 4)** 2/4 meter.

## Chapter Seven Evaluation

Answers to Questions on page 109:

- *First Bullet:  Matching*
  **(1)** E natural minor; **(2)** B melodic minor; **(3)** B natural minor; **(4)** D major; **(5)** E melodic minor; **(6)** G major
- *Second Bullet:  Sight-Singing Melodies*
  Check for accuracy of pitch and rhythm while maintaining a steady beat.

## Chapter Eight Overview

In Chapter Eight, the subdominant chord is presented in the keys of C major and F major.  The concept of simple and compound meter is discussed, as well as the introduction of 6/8 meter.  Combinable lines and a sight-singing song reinforce the concept of 6/8 meter in the key of F major.

## Chapter Eight Focus

- Compose short pieces within specified guidelines. *(NS 4a)*
- Read notation in 6/8 meter. *(NS 5a)*
- Read at sight simple melodies in treble clef and bass clef. *(NS 5b)*

- Identify and define standard notation symbols for pitch and rhythm. *(NS 5c)*
- Use standard notation to record musical ideas. *(NS 5d)*

### Chapter Eight Evaluation
Answers to Questions on page 119.
- *First Bullet:  Name the Notes*
  The note names for the C major tonic chord are:  C, E, G, C or *do, mi, sol, do.*  The note names for the F major tonic chord are:  F, A, C, F or *do, mi, sol, do.*  The note names for the C major dominant chord are:  G, B, D, G or *sol, ti, re, sol.*  The note names for the F major dominant chord are:  C, E, G, C or *sol, ti, re, sol.*  The note names for the C major subdominant chord are:  F, A, C, F or *fa, la, do, fa.*  The note names for the F major subdominant chord are:  B♭, D, F, B♭ or *fa, la, do, fa.*
- *Second Bullet:  Sight-Singing Melodies*
  Check for accuracy of pitch and rhythm while maintaining a steady beat.

### Chapter Eight Evaluation
Answers to Questions on page 120.
- *First Bullet:  Simple or Compound Meter?*
  Simple meter phrases 1, 3, 5; Compound meter phrases 2, 4, 6.
- *Second Bullet:  Sight-Singing Melody*
  Check for accurate pitch and rhythm while maintaining a steady beat.
- *Third Bullet:  Be A Composer*
  Each composition will be different.  Check for correct rhythms.  Provide students the opportunity to play their compositions on rhythm instruments. The opportunity to add pitches and transfer to a staff will require a review for accuracy of key choice, notes, and rhythm patterns.

## Chapter Nine Overview
In Chapter Nine, the B♭ major scale, tonic chord, dominant chord, and subdominant chord are presented in exercises and combinable lines.  The rhythmic concept of syncopation and the music symbol for accent is introduced.  Sight-singing songs in the key of B♭ provide practice in 6/8 meter and syncopation.

### Chapter Nine Focus
- Read notation in 6/8 meter. Read syncopation in 3/4 and 4/4 meters. *(NS 5a)*
- Read at sight simple melodies in treble clef and bass clef. *(NS 5b)*
- Identify and define standard notation symbols for pitch, rhythm and articulation. *(NS 5c)*

### Chapter Nine Evaluation
Answers to Questions on page 132:
- *First Bullet:  Major Keys*
  **(1)** Tonic chord: *do, mi, sol;* **(2)** Dominant chord:  *sol, ti, re;* **(3)** Subdominant chord: *fa, la, do.*
- *Second Bullet:  Sight-Singing Exercise*
  Check for accurate pitch and rhythm while maintaining a steady beat.
- *Third Bullet:  Answer the Questions*
  **(1)** accent; **(2)** syncopation
- *Fourth Bullet:  Sight-Singing Exercise*
  Check for accurate pitch and rhythm while maintaining a steady beat.

## Chapter Ten Overview
In Chapter Ten, the G minor scale, tonic chord, dominant chord, and subdominant chord are presented in exercises and combinable lines.  Borrowed division is defined, including examples of duplets and triplets. Additional examples of simple meter and cut time are introduced.  Sight-singing songs in G minor and E♭ major are included.

### Chapter Ten Focus
- Compose short pieces within specified guidelines. *(NS 4a)*
- Read notation including duplets and triplets. *(NS 5a)*

- Read at sight simple melodies in treble and bass clef. (NS 5b)
- Identify and define standard notation symbols for pitch, rhythm and tempo. (NS 5c)
- Use standard notation to record musical ideas. (NS 5d)

## Chapter Ten Evaluation
Answers to Questions on page 146:
- *Answer the Questions*
  **(1)** B♭ major scale; **(2)** B♭ and E♭; **(3)** The note names for the G minor tonic chord are: G, B♭, D or *la, do, mi*; the note names for the G minor dominant chord are: D, F, A, D or *mi, sol, ti, mi*; the note names for the G minor subdominant chord are: C, E♭, G, C or *re, fa, la, re*.
- *Second Bullet: Simple or Compound Meter?*
  **(1)** simple meter; **(2)** compound meter
- *Third Bullet: Be A Composer*
  Each composition will be different. Check for correct rhythm patterns in both the simple and compound meter writing exercises. Provide students the opportunity to play their compositions on rhythm instruments. The opportunity to add pitches and transfer to a staff will require a review for accuracy of key choice, notes and rhythm patterns.

# Chapter Eleven Overview
In Chapter Eleven, the C minor and A major scales, tonic chords, dominant chords, and subdominant chords are presented in exercises, combinable lines, and sight-singing songs. Altered pitches and accidentals including the sharp, flat and natural are presented. The altered pitch names in solfège syllables are also introduced. Rhythmic examples in 3/8, 6/8, 9/8 and 12/8 meter are included. Diatonic and chromatic scales are presented along with modes and modal scales in exercises and a sight-singing song.

## Chapter Eleven Focus
- Read notation in various meters. (NS 5a)
- Read at sight simple melodies in treble clef and bass clef. (NS 5b)
- Identify and define standard notation for pitch and rhythm. (NS 5c)

## Chapter Eleven Evaluation
Answers to Questions on page 173:
- *First Bullet: Simple Meter*
  Answers can vary. A question mark equals one beat, so check for accuracy of rhythm pattern choice.
- *Second Bullet: Compound Meter Questions*
  Answers can vary. A question mark equals one beat, so check for accuracy of rhythm pattern choice.
- *Third Bullet: Chromatic Pitches*
  Check for accuracy of chromatic pitches and rhythm while maintaining a steady beat.

## Chapter Eleven Evaluation
Answers to Questions on page 174:
- *First Bullet: Answer the Questions*
  **(1)** sharp; **(2)** flat; **(3)** natural; **(4)** accidental and altered pitch
- *Second Bullet: Name the Notes and Sing the Scales*
  **(a)** D Dorian scale: D, E, F, G, A, B, C , D or *re, mi, fa, sol, la, ti, do, re*; **(b)** D Mixolydian scale: D, E, F♯, G, A, B, C, D or *sol, la, ti, do re, mi, fa, sol*.
- *Third Bullet: Sight-Singing Melody*
  Check for accurate pitch and rhythm in the Dorian modal exercise.

# Chapter Twelve Overview
In Chapter Twelve the Circle of Fifths is introduced. Scales, tonic chords, dominant chords and subdominant chords are presented in the following keys: A♭ major, F minor, D♭ major, B♭ minor, G♭ major, E♭ minor, E major, C♯ minor, B major, G♯ minor,

F# major and D# minor. Practice drills and combinable line exercises are given for each key.

## Chapter Twelve Focus
- Read at sight simple melodies in treble clef and bass clef. *(NS 5b)*
- Identify and define standard notation symbols for pitch. *(NS 5c)*

## Chapter Twelve Evaluation
Answers to Questions on page 200:
- *First Bullet: Answer the Questions*
  **(1)** three; **(2)** one; **(3)** four
- *Second Bullet: Sight-Singing Melodies*
  "Did You See..." is in the key of C# minor.
  "Got a Flat Tire!" is in the key of A♭ major
  "Always Trust..." is in the key of B♭ minor.
  Check for accuracy of pitch and rhythm while maintaining a steady beat.

# Pitch

◆ **Sight-Singing Method • Movable *Do* in Major Keys**
Regardless of the key, *do* is always the first pitch of the scale.

◆ **Diatonic Scales**

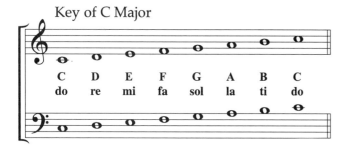

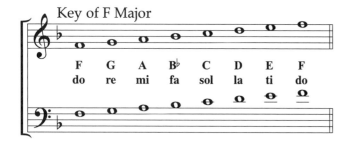

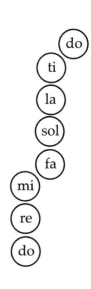

◆ **Chromatic Scales**

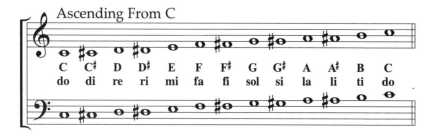

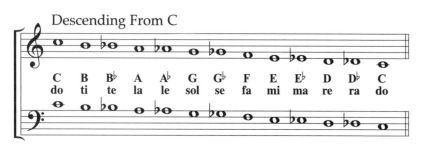

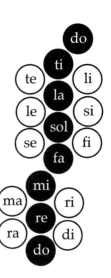

# Pitch

◆ **Sight-Singing Method • Movable *Do* in Minor Keys**
Regardless of the key, *la* is always the first pitch of the scale.

◆ **The Natural Minor Scale**

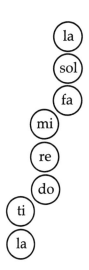

◆ **The Harmonic Minor Scale**

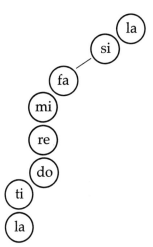

◆ **The Melodic Minor Scale**

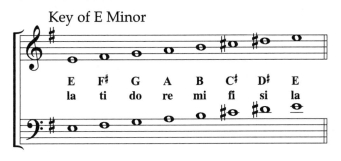

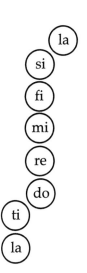

# Pitch

## ◆ Sight-Singing Method • Fixed *Do* in Major Keys
Regardless of the key, *do* is always C.

## ◆ Diatonic Scales

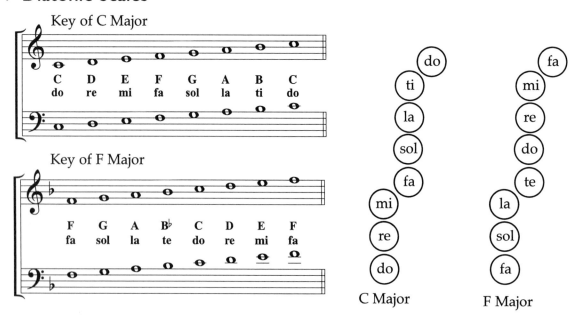

## ◆ Chromatic Scales

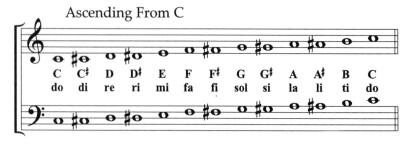

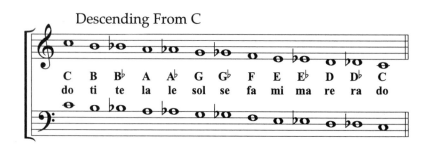

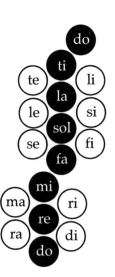

# Pitch

### ◆ Sight-Singing Method • Fixed *Do* in Minor Keys

Regardless of the key, *la* is always A.

### ◆ The Natural Minor Scale

Key of A Minor

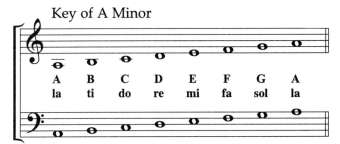

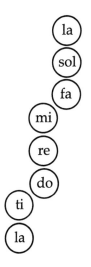

### ◆ The Harmonic Minor Scale

Key of D Minor

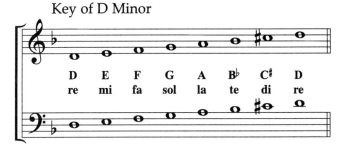

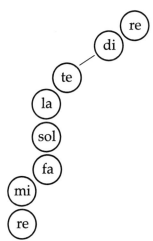

### ◆ The Melodic Minor Scale

Key of E Minor

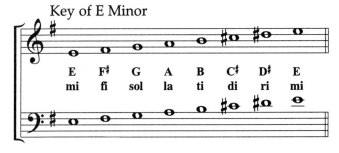

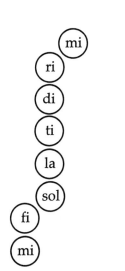

# Pitch

## ◆ Sight-Singing Method • Numbers in Major Keys

Regardless of the key, "1" is always the first pitch of the scale.

## ◆ Diatonic Scales

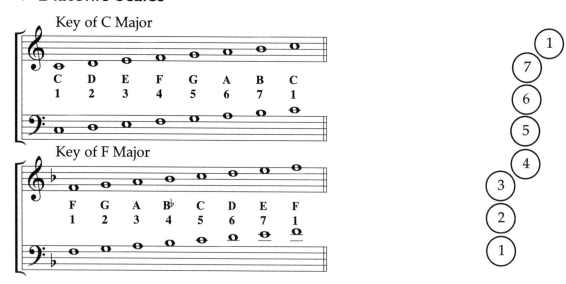

Accidentals can be performed either by singing the number but raising or lowering the pitch by a half step, or by singing the word "sharp" or "flat" before the number as a grace note.

## ◆ Chromatic Scales

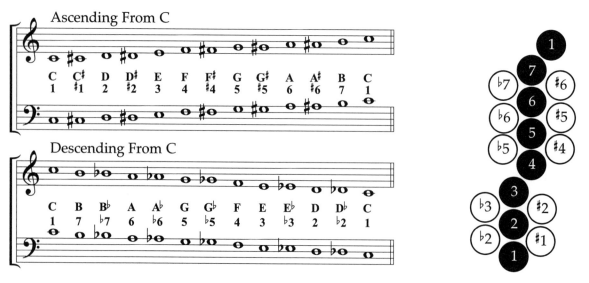

# Pitch

◆ ## Sight-Singing Method • Numbers in Minor Keys
Regardless of the key, "6" is always the first pitch of the scale.

◆ ## The Natural Minor Scale

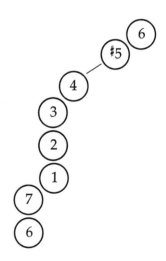

◆ ## The Harmonic Minor Scale

◆ ## The Melodic Minor Scale

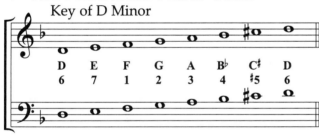

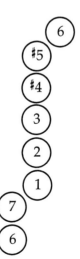

# Rhythm

## ◆ Counting Methods • Simple Meter

Following are three methods in use for counting rhythms in simple meter.

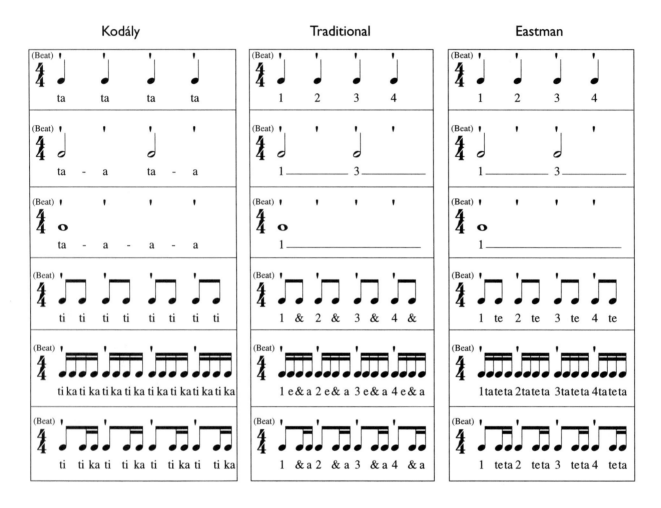

# Rhythm

◆ Counting Methods • Simple Meter

# Rhythm

## ◆ Counting Methods • Compound Meter

Following are three methods in use for counting rhythms in compound meter.

| Kodály | Traditional | Eastman |
|:---:|:---:|:---:|
| 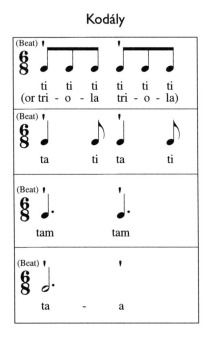 | 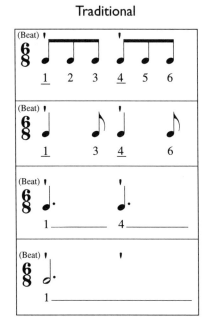 | 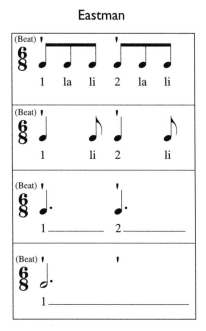 |

# Practice

### ◆ Rhythm • Simple Meter
Clap, tap, or chant while conducting the following exercises.

Exercises Based on the Beat

Exercises Based on the Division of the Beat

Exercises Based on the Subdivision of the Beat

# Practice

◆ Rhythm • Dotted Notes

Clap, tap, or chant while conducting the following exercises.

Exercises with Dotted Half Notes

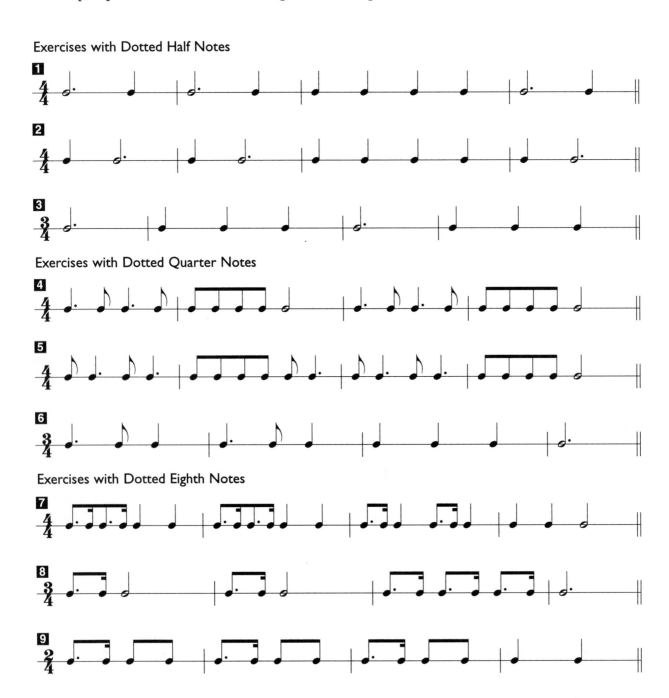

Exercises with Dotted Quarter Notes

Exercises with Dotted Eighth Notes

# Practice

## ◆ Rhythm • Compound Meter

Clap, tap, or chant while conducting the following exercises.

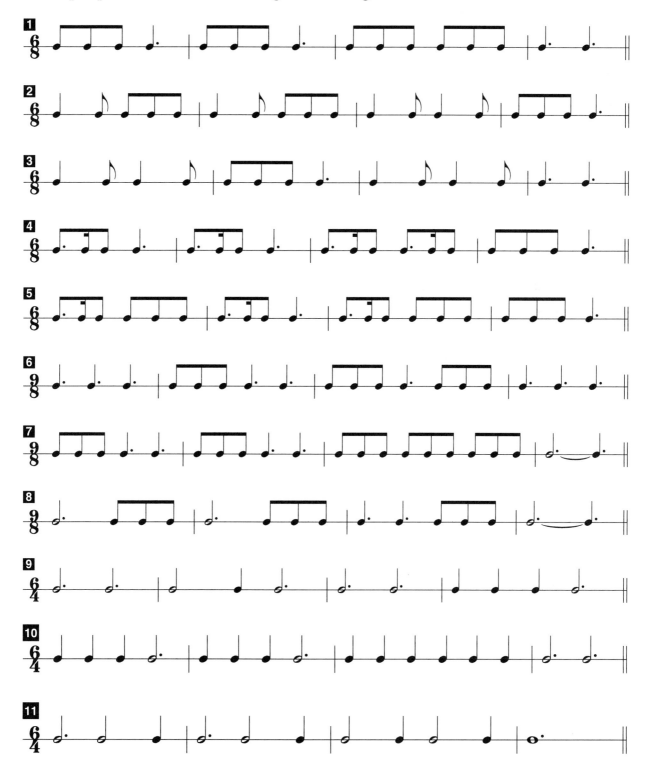

# Pitch

## ◆ The Circle of Fifths

In music, the relationship between each key is based on a perfect fifth. A **perfect fifth** is *an interval of two pitches that are five notes apart on the staff.* An easy way to visualize this relationship is on the keyboard.

Study the keyboard below. Notice that if you start on C and move to the left by the distance of a fifth, you will find the keys that contain flats. Notice that the number of flats in each key signature increases by one each time you move one perfect fifth to the left.

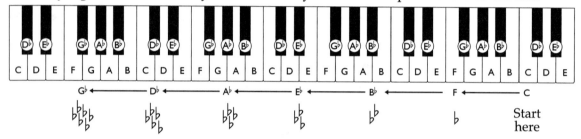

However, if you start on C and move to the right by the distance of a fifth, you will find the keys that contain sharps. Notice that the number of sharps in each key signature increases by one each time you move one perfect fifth to the right.

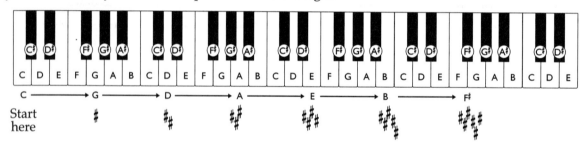

The Circle of Fifths is another easy way to visualize and memorize patterns of sharps, flats and key signatures.

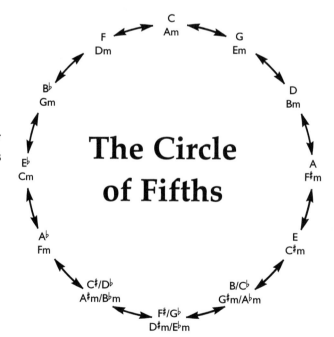

# Pitch

◆ ## The Piano Keyboard

For use with Sight-Singing exercises. Use the keyboard and notation on this page to identify and perform the notes in your voice part.

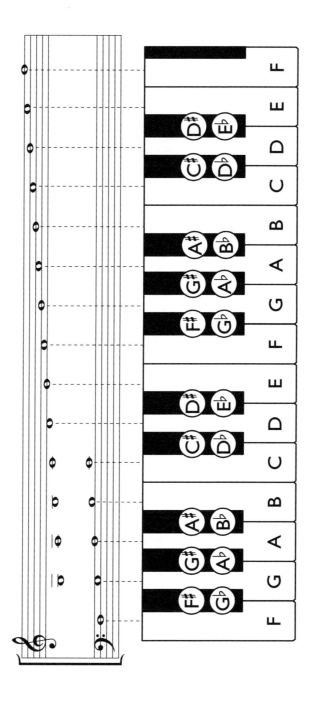